Destination Unknown

Engaging with the problems
of marginalised youth

Tom Bentley and Ravi Gurumurthy

DEM☉S

First published in 1999
Reprinted in 2000

by Demos
Elizabeth House
39 York Road
London SE1 7NQ
tel: 020 7401 5330
fax: 020 7401 5331
email: mail@demos.co.uk

ISBN 1 898309 29 9

Printed in Great Britain by Redwood Books
Design by Lindsay Nash

DEM⊙S

WITHDRAWN

Demos is an independent think tank committed to radical thinking on the long-term problems facing the UK and other advanced industrial societies.

It aims to develop ideas – both theoretical and practical – to help shape the politics of the twenty first century, and to improve the breadth and quality of political debate.

Demos publishes books and a regular journal and undertakes substantial empirical and policy oriented research projects. Demos is a registered charity.

In all its work Demos brings together people from a wide range of backgrounds in business, academia, government, the voluntary sector and the media to share and cross-fertilise ideas and experiences.

For further information and
subscription details please contact:
Demos
Elizabeth House
39 York Road
London SE1 7NQ
tel: 020 7401 5330
fax: 020 7401 5331
email: mail@demos.co.uk
www.demos.co.uk

Other publications by Demos:

The Real Deal: What young people really think about government, politics and social exclusion

The Wealth and Poverty of Networks (Demos Collection 12)

The Family in Question

Relative Values: Support for relationships and parenting

Freedom's Children: Work, relationships and politics for 18-34 year olds in Britain today

Contents

About the authors

Tom Bentley is Director of Demos.

Ravi Gurumurthy, formerly a researcher at Demos, is now Policy Assistant to the Head of the Social Exclusion Unit.

Acknowledgements

This research project was made possible by the financial support and partnership of the Camelot Foundation. The Carnegie United Kingdom Trust provided additional support. Thanks also go to our partners in the Real Deal, a separate but parallel consultation project with fourteen to 24 year olds across the UK.

We are grateful to many people for their advice, suggestions and support in completing this research project. They include: Howard Williamson, Rob Smith, Geoff Mulgan, Jon Bright, John Graham, Rex Hall, David Holloway, Victor Adebowale, John Elliott, Kylie Kilgour, Andy Gibson, Virginia Morrow, Lindsay Nash, Debbie Porter, Richard Warner and Ian Christie.

Paul Gregg, Jane Edgeley and Kirstine Hanson provided invaluable help and support in analysing the data. Husna Mortuza and George Lawson both carried out extensive research during the project which contributed greatly to the overall findings and analysis. Debbie Porter, Lindsay Nash and Tom Hampson were all indispensable. Ben Jupp, Kim Seltzer and Gavin Mensah-Coker provided many suggestions and improvements to the text.

We would also like to thank the many projects we visited for their time and enthusiasm. Finally, the young people involved in the Real Deal consultation were a constant source of insight and explanation of the issues facing them, as well as of encouragement and motivation.

Introduction

A new problem

This report examines a poorly understood problem that, until now, has not been seriously considered by national policy-makers in the UK. Hundreds of thousands of young people are currently 'off-register': not in full-time education, training or employment and not claiming unemployment-related benefits. Despite a sharper focus on young people, government and public service providers do not have the knowledge, the tools or the frameworks to deal effectively with this problem. In fact, the way that the system operates has actively contributed to it over the past fifteen years.

This might seem surprising. After all, youth policy and young people have become a high government and social priority. Three out of five of the Labour Party's pre-election pledges were about children and young people. Education services are receiving significant increases in real spending. The New Deal for the young unemployed is a huge public investment, aiming to eliminate long-term youth unemployment as a problem. But the message of this report is that, because the frameworks that we use to provide services and support are flawed, too many people are falling outside them. Increasing spending and effort on what happens *within* the system is not enough to reach and support them. Leaving them where they are will incur serious costs, both to their individual life chances and to society as a whole.

The report focuses on the identities and needs of these young people and the policy responses that can support them in achieving safe, independent, adult lifestyles. But policies are only effective when they fit the external conditions in which they are deployed. The root of the problem lies in the effects of change in the wider social, economic and cultural climate. Many are struggling to adapt to these changes, relying on support frameworks and institutions that are now ill-suited to the challenges they are trying to meet.

This chapter sets out the broad changes of the past twenty years in the main spheres of activity for young people, and the experiences and circumstances that put their long-term futures at greatest risk. While many are surviving and thriving in this new context, too many are not. The institutions and support mechanisms available work reasonably well only for those at the higher end of the spectrum of educational attainment. While there has always been inequality of opportunity in British society, in previous generations there have also been reliable structures through which people have gained the chance to achieve stable employment, secure family lives and the prospect of individual self-reliance. For too many, such structures no longer work. It is this loss of clear pathways which presents the greatest cause for concern.

Chapter two outlines the extent and nature of the problem. We reveal the first national picture of young people not in work, full-time education and training, or claiming unemployment benefits. In chapters three and four we consider what can be done setting out the range of risks and resources and drawing on case studies, consultation, and evidence from abroad. Chapter five sets out a new policy framework to meet the needs of all young people.

The context: changing routes to adulthood

The transition from child to adulthood has been reshaped in recent decades by a combination of economic, demographic and cultural changes. New risks and new polarities have emerged as key sectors of society have been restructured.

Economic structure and employment

The transition from education to employment is at the heart of growing up. It signals a fundamental shift towards independence, security and adulthood. But in a relatively short period, this transition has changed substantially, both in the amount of time it takes to make it and in the final destination. The transformation of the UK's underlying economic structure, as in other developed countries, has had a profound effect. It has changed not just the timing and conditions of the transition, but also the kinds of knowledge which young people need to acquire and apply, and the organisational and cultural frameworks that help to structure their routines and aspirations. The key changes are:

- a shift towards economic sectors based on knowledge and services; employment in heavy industrial, primary and manufacturing industries has dwindled steadily and will continue to decline
- rising premium on skills, work experience and 'human capital'
- increasing participation by women in the labour force, rising by 26 per cent since 1976 to 12.3 million; by 2002, women are projected to make up the majority of workers

- changing work routines: continued growth of part-time, temporary and self-employment; between 1986 and 1996 part-time employment rose from 21 per cent to 29 per cent of the workforce.

These changes have a particularly direct effect on young people. They are of less concern for those still participating in education, since they are more likely to find secure and high-wage jobs later on in life. However, for those who leave school early with few qualifications, the experience of intermittent employment in poorly paid jobs or exclusion from employment altogether is a great danger. For those who leave school at sixteen, the risk of ending up in the following spring without either a full-time job or a place on government-supported training has increased from one in ten in 1989 to more than one in three in 1996.[1] A recent survey of jobs undertaken by young people aged sixteen and seventeen who left school without five GCSEs above grade C and who are currently in work but not in formal training showed that the young men were most often employed in labouring, assembly, packing or sorting work in factories or warehouses, while the women were also doing relatively low-skilled jobs such as assembly work, retail assistants and waitressing jobs.[2] The work on offer in such industries is less likely to lead to occupational security or stable incomes than the equivalent jobs of a generation ago.

While the work on offer to many who leave school at sixteen provides a less stable environment for the transition to adulthood, many school leavers do not even have that. Youth unemployment has been roughly twice the national average for almost two decades. Between 1990 and 1997, overall unemployment rose by just over 1 per cent, while the number of unemployed sixteen to nineteen year olds rose from 13 per cent to 18 per cent.[3]

In the last quarter of 1998, at a time of record employment levels, seasonally adjusted unemployment for sixteen and seventeen year olds was 18 per cent and 11 per cent for eighteen to 24 year olds – both well above the rates for other age groups.

Some argue that youth unemployment should not cause too much concern because most young people are unemployed for a short period of time. Nearly 40 per cent of eighteen to 24 year olds who start claiming the Jobseeker's Allowance have stopped after two months, while only a quarter of current claimants have claimed for six months or longer. But this apparent mobility obscures a more worrying feature. Our research shows that two-thirds of all new benefit claimants aged between eighteen and 24 have claimed before in the past two years. A third have claimed on two or more occasions. For many young people, entering the labour market at its margins does not lead to greater security later on. A cycle of 'low pay, no pay' has become the dominant feature of many local labour markets for young workers with few skills. One bridge to adult independence – secure income, enhanced skills and status through steady work – has been significantly weakened.

Education

Alongside huge changes in employment, the educational landscape has also been transformed. The picture is of rising achievement and participation for most, which has made the persistent minority who fail relatively more disadvantaged.

Overall, young people are significantly more likely to have qualifications than their elders: only 27 per cent of nineteen to 21 year olds do not have a qualification equivalent to five high grade GCSEs compared with 38 per cent for people of all ages.[4] Forty-six per cent of fifteen year old pupils gained five or more GCSEs at Grade C in 1998.[5] In many subjects girls have overtaken boys, with half of all females getting five or more high grade GCSEs compared with two in five males.[6]

This rise in achievement has been accompanied by a rapid expansion of further and higher education over the past two decades. Government and individuals alike have realised that access to employment is increasingly dependent on post-sixteen qualifications. Nearly 75 per cent of sixteen to eighteen year olds now stay in some form of education or training compared to 60 per cent ten years ago. Full-time education in particular has boomed. The number of seventeen year olds in England attending school or college full time has increased from below 24 per cent in 1979 to 57 per cent in 1998.[7] The number of eighteen year olds in full-time education has more than doubled in the last ten years to 38 per cent.[8] One in three people now enter higher education, three times the number in 1970.

But while many are achieving more than their parents' generation, for others the choices and risks have become more stark. Earnings differentials between those with and without qualifications continue to grow in an increasingly knowledge-based economy. A worker with A level or equivalent qualifications earns on average 25 per cent more than one with no qualifications at all. While 3.9 per cent of men who had entered higher education were unemployed in August 1997, 15.6 per cent of those with no qualifications were jobless. Longitudinal comparison of cohorts born in 1958 and 1970 shows that young people with poor educational attainment or poor basic skills found entry into the labour market in the 1980s much more difficult than their counterparts twelve years before.

Given the fact that the majority are now achieving more and participating longer, those who have not kept pace with this trend are relatively more disadvantaged. Although GCSE attainment has risen considerably, less than half of all sixteen year olds get five or more GCSEs at Grade C or above, with a quarter only getting one GCSE at below grade C. Almost 7 per cent of the age group get no GCSEs at all.[9] Worse still, according the OECD, the UK is one of the few countries in the developed world where young adults find it harder to read and understand newspapers and brochures than those aged 30 to 40.[10]

Full-time education and work are not mutually exclusive in the way they were once assumed to be: 10 per cent of full-time students were economically active in 1997 compared with 1 per cent in 1984.[11] University courses increasingly contain an element of work experience, while many young people supplement their courses with part-time and holiday work. Whatever one thinks of students having to work, universities at least are recognising that some contact with the labour market helps the transition to full-time employment.

Yet while further and higher education can create a smoother transition to work, for some it ends all too abruptly. While participation continues to rise, so do drop-out rates. The numbers of students failing to complete university, college and training courses creates huge costs and disrupts the paths of many young people. Several factors seem to be influential, particularly financial and emotional pressures. Some students are dropping out for positive reasons, for example, finding work or making alternative choices. But for many it is a negative experience and one that makes it even harder to navigate a safe passage. A recent study of drop-outs in post-sixteen colleges found that almost a fifth of students enrolling for A level courses did not sit their final exams.[12] This rose to 40 per cent for those who only enrolled for a single A level. Those closest to the edges of the education system seem to be most at risk of losing their way.

Family life
Alongside these changes in external conditions, family life has undergone profound changes. Two key risks emerge from the broad picture:

- some families are unable to provide the support necessary to meet young people's needs
- the process of forming partnerships and families is now marked by diversity, contingency and choice: while helpful to many people, this also adds new uncertainty and risk.

Many young people today have grown up with wide-ranging experience of family forms and relationships. While support can be provided in a range of family structures, some are more closely associated with insecurity than others. One in four children born in the 1970s experienced the break-up of their parent's marriage by the time they were aged sixteen.[13] One in twelve children currently live in step-parent families and approximately one in five children live in single parent families, three times the number in 1971.[14]

These changes have come at a time when young people are increasingly dependent on their parents until later in life, as the transitions to employment, marriage and leaving home are delayed. While many parents are able to provide the necessary emotional and financial support, for some young people family life no longer cushions the entry into adulthood.

In addition to insecurity within the parental home, young people's own relationships are also more characterised by instability. The traditional passage from single to couple to family is still made by many young people, but in general this takes longer and is accompanied by a wider range of other experiences. While most people still get married, between 1971 and 1995 the average age of first marriage rose from 23 to 26 for women, and from 25 to 28 for men. Cohabitation prior to marriage is now the norm: two thirds of couples who married in 1994 previously cohabited, compared to just one in eight twenty years before.[15] The number of first marriages has fallen steadily since the 1960s, with 40 per cent fewer first marriages in 1994 than in 1971. Once in place, these relationships are far less permanent and secure. The divorce rate among sixteen to 24 year olds was three times higher in 1995 than in 1971 as a proportion of those married. As a result of these changes the number of single person households has increased dramatically. One in four households were single person in 1997, twice the number in 1961.

Patterns of childbirth, another traditional marker of adulthood, have also undergone significant change. Overall, women are giving birth to fewer children, later in life. The average number of live births has been fairly stable since the 1980s. However, the average age of first childbirth has risen from 24.6 in 1981 to 26.5 in 1994. Although women aged 25 to 29 are still the most likely to give birth, since 1992 those aged 30 to 34 have been more likely to give birth than those aged twenty to 24. While only 16 per cent of those born in 1944 were childless at age 30, over 38 per cent of those born in 1964 have no children. Yet the averages conceal a more diverse picture. For example, the number of under sixteens conceiving has risen over the last few years. As women marry less, work more and have children at a wider range of ages, the traditional patterns of family formation have become less common and less significant.

As in education and employment, these changes represent freedom and opportunity for many and risk for a significant minority. For many young men facing insecure and low-status labour markets, the traditional roles, supports and structures of family cannot be relied upon. For women, teenage pregnancy has become one of the risk indicators of longer-term social exclusion. Lone parenthood is also often concurrent with poverty: of 1.7 million lone parents, 1 million are on income support while 0.3 million are on family credit.[16, 17]

Leaving home and homelessness

Living at home can be a source of support while young people negotiate other changes. Patterns of leaving home have changed considerably.

The point which young people leave has been delayed for many by later marriage, extended study, unemployment and low pay. Fifty-four per cent of men and 36 per cent of women aged twenty to 24 still lived with their parents in 1995.[18] The nature of leaving has also changed. Fewer are leaving permanently for marriage. The growth in numbers entering higher education has seen young people living away from home as students, returning after graduation and then leaving home permanently.[19] The process becomes more reversible and protracted: a less abrupt change. For most, it reflects a more complex process of development and activity, including extended educational participation, longer dependence on partial family support and periods of part-time and temporary employment to support study or fit in between study periods. For some, the transition has become smoother.

Again, however, for the most vulnerable, leaving home is now more risky. Leaving home before the age of eighteen is most often triggered by earlier problems – pregnancy, parental or own unemployment, family conflict or living with a step-parent.[20] One survey showed that the most common reason for leaving home at sixteen was problems with family.[21] Whatever the background factors, there is little doubt that early independence has become more dangerous. If it is not the conclusion of a well-supported period of preparation and transition, leaving home will often precipitate a cycle of experiences and risks that do long-term harm to individual life chances.

For some young people who leave home early, the effect on their life chances can be still worse. Although accurate figures are difficult to come by, research suggests that youth homelessness has increased significantly. Young people may end up homeless for a variety of reasons, but in particular it is associated with intense family conflict and abuse. Most strikingly, research suggests that one in three young homeless people have experience of local authority care. The profile of young homeless people consistently shows that this group has multiple and linked problems such as alcohol and drug abuse, no qualifications, mental health problems, family conflict and experience of care or prison.[22] Research also suggests that increasing numbers of homeless are coming from younger age groups, particularly sixteen and seventeen year olds, which may be partly connected to this age group's reduced housing and unemployment benefit entitlements and diminishing opportunities of work.[23]

Social exclusion

The emergence of increased risk in individual spheres such as education and employment is part of a wider process affecting the whole of society: the concentration of social and economic deprivation *geographically,* and the heightening of income and *life chance inequality.* Almost one-fifth of working-age households have no family member earning an income. People living in the poorest fifth of local wards are more than two and a half times more likely to be unemployed than those living in the best-off fifth. A 1995 survey of secondary schools serving 'difficult to let' estates found that one in four children gained no GCSEs, five times the national rate, and that truancy was four times the national average.[24]

This concentration of opportunity and disadvantage also accentuates the point that, within national averages, local conditions, cultures and resources help to shape young people's transitions. Access to employment is particularly marked by geographical variations. For instance in August 1997, Cleveland, Merseyside and South Yorkshire had unemployment rates of 9 to 10 per cent while Surrey, Berkshire and Hertfordshire had rates of 2 to 3 per cent.[25] Within smaller areas, the disparities are sometimes even greater: in 1991, while the national unemployment rate was 9 per cent, unemployment in the ten most deprived local authority districts such as Hackney and Knowsley ranged from 17 to 23 per cent. Location determines not only chances of employment but often access to cheaper food, banks, health provision and entertainment.

Much of the social exclusion debate has focused on urban problems. But it is important to note that many rural areas have a combination of linked problems such as poor transport, lack of access to shops and banks, lack of affordable housing and unemployment. A recent study of twelve rural areas showed that at least 20 per cent of households in nine of the areas were in, or on the margins, of poverty. More than 90 per cent of parishes did not have a bank or a building society, 70 per cent did not have a store and 80 per cent did not have a GP surgery, while 75 per cent of parishes did not have a daily bus service.[26]

Overall, the concentration of disadvantage into specific geographical areas and social groups helps to compound the difficulty that many young people already face in making positive steps towards adulthood. Alongside the lack of material resources, mobility and straightforward information about opportunities, there are also less tangible factors such as the absence of strong, positive, adult role models.

Crime

Young people aged sixteen to 24 are by far the most likely to be the victims of crime. A quarter of all violent offences in Britain are committed against young men aged sixteen to 24. Part of the reason why young people are more at risk is their greater likelihood of being unemployed, on a low income, or living in rented housing in inner cities or in run-down areas. While on average 6 per cent of all households were the victims of burglary, 15 per cent of households headed by people aged sixteen to 24 were victims, while for young people heading households in inner cities, the figure is 19.3 per cent.

But young people are also the most likely to be the perpetrators of crime. Two out of every five offenders in 1994 were under 21 and one in four were under eighteen.

While most young people's involvement in crime was either non-existent or relatively fleeting, 3 per cent of offenders are responsible for 25 per cent of all crimes committed. For a small but growing number of young people, offending leads to imprisonment. The population of young offenders under sentence, which fell by half between 1980 and 1993, has risen by 30 per cent in the three years to 1996.

Unsurprisingly, many young offenders share a cluster of similar characteristics and experiences. Many have either truanted or been excluded from school, have no qualifications and have lived in the care system. Recent research by the Metropolitan Police identified those who either truant or are excluded from school as being responsible for 40 per cent of all street robberies and a third of car thefts and burglaries in London. Over half of all prisoners under the age of eighteen have been in care. Almost two-thirds have no qualifications and the same proportion were unemployed before conviction. Almost a quarter are fathers or expectant fathers. Over half of young prisoners on remand have a diagnosable mental disorder. Up to a quarter admit to having a current or past drink problem but almost three-quarters say they have never received any help with their problems. Seventeen per cent admit to having suffered abuse of a violent, sexual or emotional nature. One in ten admit to self-harm.[27] These shocking statistics demonstrate the extent to which the problems faced by those young people most at risk are interconnected.

While each sphere of life or activity has its own particular features, the consequences of adversity, disadvantage or failure can produce a set of circumstances that becomes depressingly familiar. In the case of crime, they also demonstrate the huge cost to families, communities and society as a whole.

One of the most disheartening trends is that the transition out of crime appears to be occurring later and with little help from the state. The peak age of offending rose from sixteen in 1986 to eighteen in 1994. And while most do stop, conviction and punishment does little to improve the offending patterns of many. Three out of four offenders under 21 sentenced to prison in 1993 were reconvicted within two years of being discharged and 68 per cent of those doing community service also re-offended.

Well-being

The increase in both pressure and opportunity for younger members of the population is also reflected in long-term changes in levels of well-being. Between 1980 and 1990, suicides increased by 85 per cent among men aged fifteen to 24, and by a third among 25 to 44 year olds. Specific factors such as homelessness, unemployment, drug misuse, mental illness and lack of social support are particularly associated with suicide. Other triggers can be stressful life events such as job loss, bereavement or relationship breakdown. Suicide is now the second most common cause of death for eighteen to 24 year olds. Other 'disorders of youth'[28] such as crime, substance use, depression and eating disorders have also risen steadily over the past 40 years.

An estimated 100,000 people each year are referred to hospitals in England and Wales for deliberate self-harm, mainly involving drug overdoses or self-injury. One-fifth of these are young people. A survey of female self-injurers for the Bristol Crisis Service for Women in 1994–95 shows that 74 per cent had begun self-injuring themselves during childhood and adolescence (up to the age of nineteen).

More generally, mental illness and depressive and emotional disorders among young people have increased significantly. Six per cent of men and 16 per cent of women aged sixteen to nineteen are thought to have some form of mental health problem. While only 2 per cent of children under the age of twelve suffer from depression, the figure rises to 5 per cent for teenagers. Many young people with mental health difficulties do not come into contact with specialist services.[29] One in four children living in inner cities will have significant mental health problems, compared with one in ten in rural areas. Other risk factors include family divorce, parental bereavement and experience of abuse or neglect. Children who have been bullied are also at greater risk of anxiety, sleep problems, depression and thoughts of suicide.

The link between homelessness and mental health problems is particularly strong. A third of homeless young people have attempted suicide and they are three times more likely than the national average to experience mental health problems, which are more likely to be chronic and severe.

Culture, values and lifestyle

The values and lifestyles of young people are a barometer for wider social change. The generations born since the 1960s have helped to strengthen the priorities of freedom, personal fulfilment and ethical concerns against the more basic post-war priorities of security, material well-being and stability. The growth of global multimedia and brand marketing have increased the pressure to consume and helped to make material differences between young people more obvious. For some, this can lead to destructive patterns of behaviour such as debt, crime and drug taking, which can which have serious consequences on people's health and well-being for the rest of their lives.

But although the potential pitfalls for young people are wider than for previous generations, most young people manage to experiment and make mistakes with relatively few serious consequences. Those who fail to navigate these risks often have a range of other characteristics which, in combination, produce particular danger.

Entitlements and responsibilities

As the contours of adolescence and youth have changed, the framework of rights, entitlements and responsibilities concerning young people has also shifted. Overall, the picture remains confused and fragmented, but key themes can be identified that may contribute to the danger of losing touch with the resources and responsibilities needed to achieve independence. The key features of a framework which has evolved almost by default are:

- a stretching of the *timeframe* in which young people assume full social and legal citizenship
- a greater focus on *individual* contribution and qualification
- growing *conditionality* of entitlements
- lack of *coherence* in the stages and frameworks young people pass through.

Many of the ways in which young people come into contact with public services, entitlements and obligations now begin earlier in life. From the younger age of criminal responsibility to the guarantee of a nursery place to three year olds, children and young people are increasingly identified as *individual* recipients of services and carriers of responsibility at younger ages. At the same time, the point at which they achieve full citizenship and entitlement has, in many ways, been pushed back. Although voting rights start at eighteen, the full rights of social citizenship – unemployment and housing benefits, social protection such as the minimum wage – do not reach their full level until the age of 25 and are increasingly predicated on individual qualification and contribution.

The principle that university students should contribute to, and pay back, the costs of their education through direct hypothecated means also reflects the growing individualisation of people's contact with the public service infrastructure. The creation of Individual Learning Accounts and Personal Job Accounts shows that the new infrastructure of lifelong learning and government service provision is set to move further in this direction.

In schooling, despite the fact that successful educational careers depend greatly on coherent progress from early to late teens, there is still a fundamental shift in the level and type of requirement at sixteen. Young people (if they are still at school) move from a system where they are legally required to attend and where most of the important choices about their learning are made for them to a system which increasingly depends on individual choice and responsibility, and where dropping out or moving between providers is easy to initiate, although often difficult to execute successfully.

Changes in the benefit system also show the growing conditionality of public service entitlements. Sixteen and seventeen year olds have been particularly affected by the withdrawal of Income Support and Housing Benefit in 1988. Its replacement, an allowance conditional on participation in government-supported training, illustrates the trend towards tying income transfers to specific behavioural conditions, also demonstrated in the conditions attached to the new Jobseeker's Allowance in 1996.

The New Deal for eighteen to 25 year olds has, in many ways, extended this principle of 'no rights without responsibilities'. While arguably increasing the opportunities available for some young unemployed people, it also imposes more conditions, particularly the duty to take up one of the four options offered at the end of the four-month gateway period. Creating structured frameworks within which to deliver a range of services and benefits is, in principle, a good idea. But one important test of effectiveness is the extent to which the framework matches the contours and realities of the situation faced by the service recipient. The danger is that such structures, if they do not fit well enough, will leave people completely outside the sphere of any service provision.

Increased stringency for sixteen to 25 year olds is not confined to unemployment-related benefits. In 1996, the amount of housing benefit was limited to a figure set by the local rent officer. Those under the age of 25 were made eligible only for the 'average local rent for bed-sit or shared accommodation'. The effect of this change was not only to reduce the amount that under 25s can claim but to encourage discrimination by landlords against young tenants, since over 25s can bear higher rents.

An important question raised by these changes, all of them *ad hoc*, some deliberate and some the by-product of reform in other areas, is the extent to which people's behaviour is shaped by the rules and conditions that public authorities set. The underlying assumption behind the removal of benefits for sixteen and seventeen year olds is that loss of benefit income would discourage leaving home and encourage participation in the system: that young people's choices would be guided by economic rationality. In a similar way, the statutory requirement to participate in education up to the age of sixteen is founded on the view that people will obey legal obligations. In both cases, these assumptions do not seem to be true for large numbers of young people. The fact that they are often the very same people whom the public and state should be most concerned to support makes the problem even more serious. From the perspective of the individual, the system appears increasingly incoherent and fragmented.

The new adolescence

In this chapter, we have seen how the contours, time horizons and challenges of growing up have changed over the past two or three decades. Access to the day-to-day reality of youth – information, opportunity, experience, expectation and risk – arrives earlier in life than it did a generation ago. But the transition to full adult status has become more protracted, involving a more complex combination of formal entitlements, investment in knowledge and other forms of personal capital, intermediate stages and contingent relationships. At the same time, many of the structures and norms that acted as props and prompts – marriage, childbirth, community structure, employment – have been weakened by wider and more general forms of change. Young people can study more, work in more skilled, challenging and mobile jobs, access information and entertainment from a vast array of sources and have more friendships and partners. But the risks of marginalisation have also grown with the increased premium on qualifications, greater burdens on increasingly unstable families and exposure to new sets of pressures and temptations.

While opportunity has increased, the responsibility for achieving real progress, of constructing meaning out of the resources and expectations on offer, seems to fall much more to the individual. For those who are equipped to thrive in these conditions, life is very promising. Many young people are achieving more than their predecessors ever expected to. But for those who start with less, who are already struggling to overcome trauma and disadvantage, whose early lives are chaotic and disrupted, and who have fewer sources of information, advice and guidance to draw on, the new landscape is threatening and insecure. As a recent comprehensive cohort study of people born in 1970 put it, the differences between those 'getting on', 'getting by' and 'getting nowhere' are increasingly stark.[30]

Put simply, it takes longer to reach full independence and maturity. Adult life can be richer, but it is also more complex, and requires more investment and longer preparation. These changes have helped to create a life stage which is profoundly different from the adolescence of the post-war generation. Although it is characterised by growing choice, experimentation and risk-taking, it is also one where individuals need a clear developmental pathway and a range of support in order to graduate to adulthood. It is marked by contingency, intermediacy and partial forms of control and independence, rather than the certainties of the life stages before and after. Despite this contingency, it has a profound influence on the direction of later life.

Because of the pace at which the change has taken place, there is now a mismatch between the needs and identities of young people and the resources and structures available to support their progress. This leads to strain and pressure on many individuals as they work their way towards their destinations. But its most dangerous consequence is the risk that some will find themselves outside the system altogether, or at best only marginally connected to it, with damaging consequences for their long-term life chances. The next chapter addresses the extent and nature of this problem.

The missing problem

Youth unemployment has been a policy concern in the UK since the early 1970s, when the labour market suffered its first major collapse for decades. At the time, many associated the problem with economic shocks and the fact that employers were retrenching in an unfriendly economic climate. Only gradually did the realisation dawn that persistently high youth unemployment was caused by changes in the underlying economic structure.

With this realisation came a new set of priorities, based primarily around the need to improve skills and qualification levels. The massive expansion of higher education in the 1980s and the creation of various youth training programmes helped to provide activity and, to some extent, obscure the problem. The growing participation of women in the labour force also contributed to the changing picture. In the 1990s, new questions arose: are young men becoming redundant before they ever get the chance to work? What are the wider skills required for employability in the modern labour market? Does the future lie in a low-skill service economy? As social concern increased, the need to make an impact on long-term unemployment among young people became more of a priority.

In the UK, the net result of this process is the New Deal for the young unemployed, the largest single social investment in the Labour government's first term and the only one for which a specific new tax was levied. The aim is straightforward: to eliminate long-term youth unemployment and raise the skill levels and employability of those young people in most need of help. The government's original target was the 250,000 young people unemployed for over six months. However, by 1997 the numbers in the claimant count had fallen significantly. Although this is partly accounted for by rising employment levels, it begs another question: are all those who are unemployed actually on the registers?

Registered unemployment is still taken by many as the key indicator of disadvantage for young people. If they are not studying or working and there is not some special reason for their being out of the labour market, such as sickness or disability, we tend to assume that young people will show up in the unemployment figures.

However, our analysis of current data shows that *for each young person claiming unemployment-related benefits there is another who is not in education, training or work and not on the register of claimant unemployment.* More than half a million sixteen to 24 year olds are not in work, full-time education or training and not claiming Jobseeker's Allowance or other unemployment-related benefits. Two-thirds of these do not even come under the accepted definition of unemployment: they are not available for and seeking work.

The danger is that these young people are at disproportionate risk of long-term marginalisation. They have characteristics which suggest that their prospects are bleak, ranging from no qualifications to living in workless households. And where others improve their prospects through education, training, the New Deal, or employment, this group are outside all of these during a formative period in their lives. The costs of this marginalisation do not just fall on them: we all pay a price for people who end up in persistent poverty, ill health and, in some cases, criminal offending. The costs to the state alone run into billions each year. For those who are parents, there are also strong intergenerational effects on the life chances of their children.

It would be wrong to assume that every single young person who falls into this group is at high risk. Some are studying part-time, some have chosen to be full-time parents and others have other reasons for not participating. But background analysis of the groups shows that, overall, we should be seriously concerned.

The data analysed here is drawn from the Labour Force Survey (LFS) – a national survey of 120,000 people aged sixteen and above. Like all household surveys, the LFS has shortcomings. It does not capture the significant numbers of young homeless people, since it contacts respondents via their permanent address. In addition, young people who are outside of mainstream provision are also disproportionately likely to be non-respondents.

Off-register

There are currently 624,000 young people aged sixteen to 24 not in work or full-time education and training and not claiming unemployment-related benefits. This figure, which excludes the long-term sick and disabled, represents one in ten of the whole age group. The overall group of young people off-register divides into five clusters:

- *sixteen to seventeen year olds: 131,000 or 21 per cent of the total off-register group*
  This group is often called 'status zero' and is treated separately because its members have different characteristics and dynamics from the off-register group

Among eighteen to 24 year olds off-register:
- *mothers and carers: 272,000 or 55 per cent of the total eighteen to 24 group*
- *the 'hidden unemployed': 125,000 or 25 per cent of the total group*
- *the 'missing': 65,000 or 13 per cent of the total group*
  Young people not in work or looking for work, not in any education or training, not carers and not long-term sick or disabled. They are economically inactive, but for no known reason. This is an underestimate because, as with all household surveys, it leaves out the young homeless
- *'marginal learners': 32,000, or 6 per cent of the total group*
  Those in part-time study but not in work, not looking for work and not on unemployment benefits.

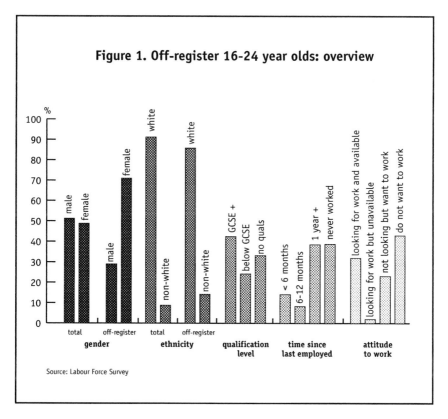

Figure 1. Off-register 16-24 year olds: overview

Source: Labour Force Survey

Marginal mothers and carers

The number of working mothers has risen dramatically over the past twenty years. In 1981, 73 per cent of mothers with children under one year old were economically inactive; by 1997, this figure had dropped to 48.4 per cent.[31] Seventy-five per cent of mothers with working partners are economically active, compared to 48 per cent of single mothers and 37 per cent of mothers with unemployed partners. Labour market participation is now the norm but is most likely among mothers who have working partners.

Young carers not in education, training or employment are not necessarily on the margins: they may simply be choosing to stay at home and look after their children. But the analysis shows that a very large proportion of this group show other characteristics associated with marginal status. As Figure 6 shows, one in three have no qualifications and one in four only have qualifications below GCSE level. A third have never worked and just 13 per cent have worked in the past year (Fig.7). Sixty-two per cent live in workless households (Fig.8).

Of the carers group, 96 per cent are female (Fig.4) and 15 per cent come from ethnic minorities, compared to 9 per cent of the general age group (Fig.5). Most carers seem to be looking after their own children rather than parents, grandparents or siblings. Ninety-six per cent of carers live in households

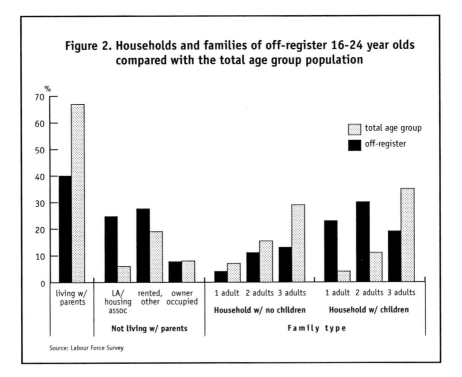

Figure 2. Households and families of off-register 16-24 year olds compared with the total age group population

Source: Labour Force Survey

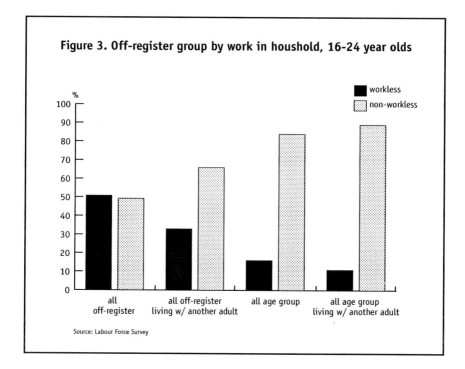

Figure 3. Off-register group by work in houshold, 16-24 year olds

Source: Labour Force Survey

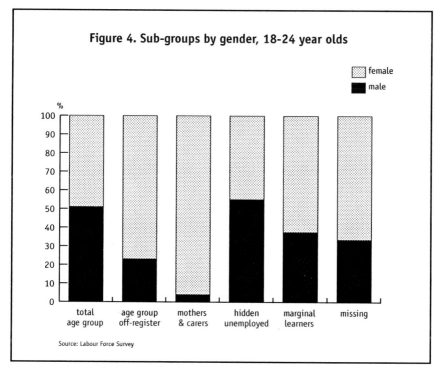

Figure 4. Sub-groups by gender, 18-24 year olds

Source: Labour Force Survey

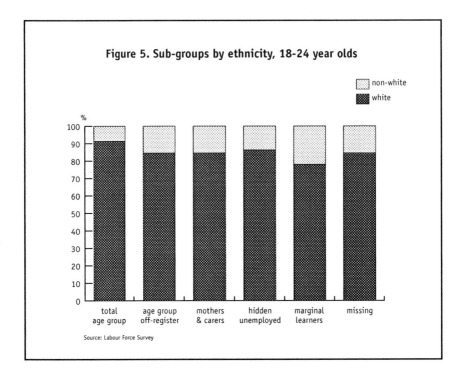

Figure 5. Sub-groups by ethnicity, 18-24 year olds

Source: Labour Force Survey

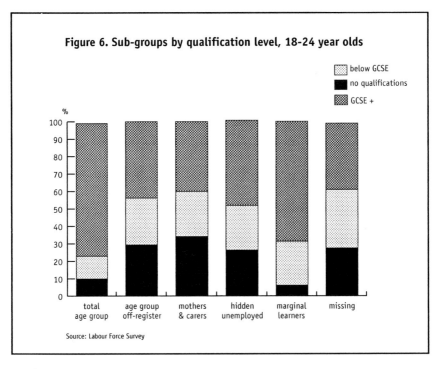

Figure 6. Sub-groups by qualification level, 18-24 year olds

Source: Labour Force Survey

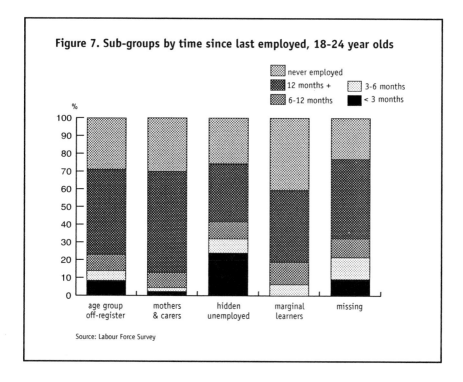

Figure 7. Sub-groups by time since last employed, 18-24 year olds

Source: Labour Force Survey

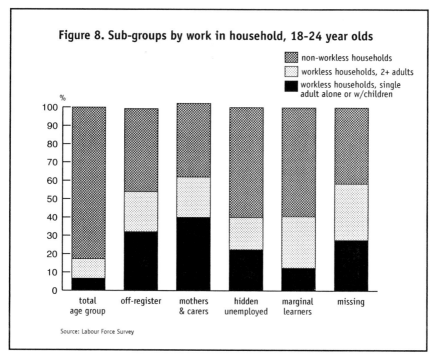

Figure 8. Sub-groups by work in household, 18-24 year olds

Source: Labour Force Survey

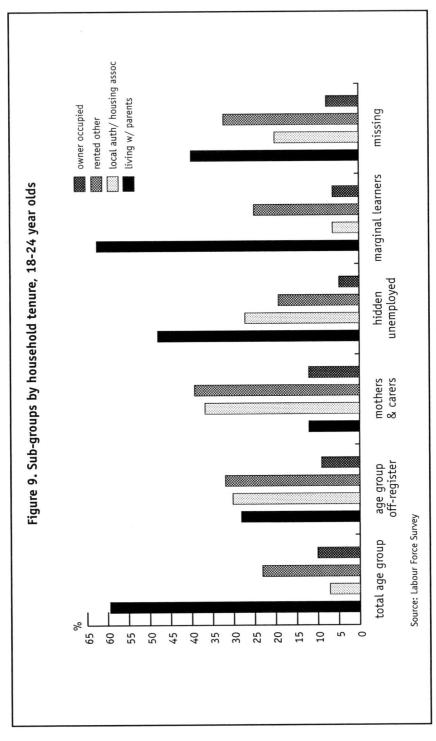

Figure 9. Sub-groups by household tenure, 18-24 year olds

Source: Labour Force Survey

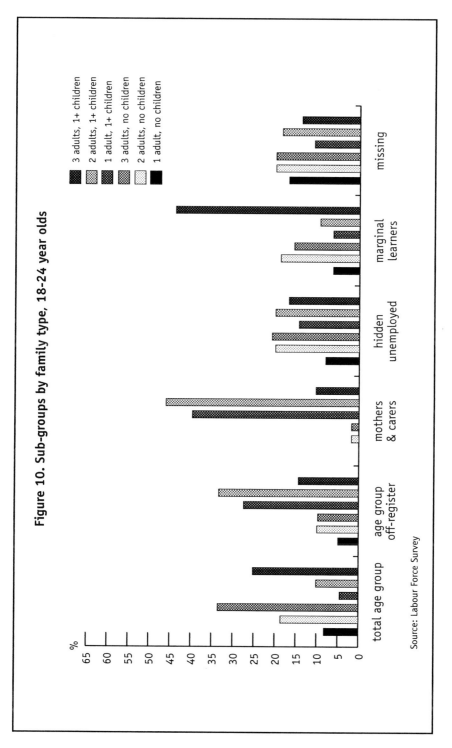

Figure 10. Sub-groups by family type, 18-24 year olds

Source: Labour Force Survey

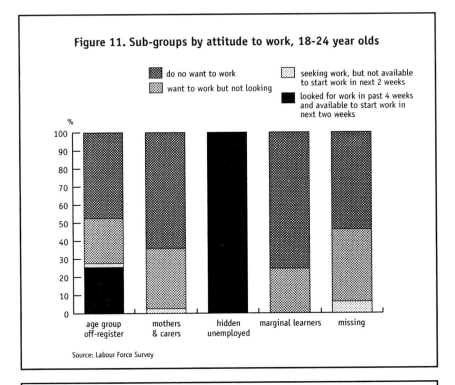

Figure 11. Sub-groups by attitude to work, 18-24 year olds

Source: Labour Force Survey

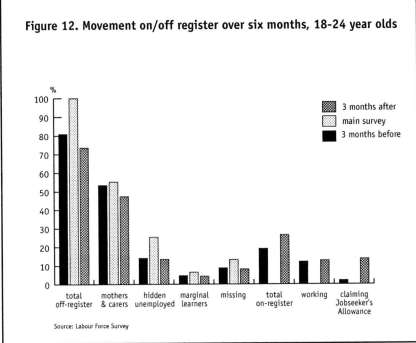

Figure 12. Movement on/off register over six months, 18-24 year olds

Source: Labour Force Survey

containing children (Fig.10) and only 12 per cent live with their parents (Fig.9).

The carers can be divided into two main groups. Single adults living with children, presumably single mothers, make up 40 per cent. Mothers living with partners or friends make up 48 per cent.

By definition, single parents who are off-register live in workless households. This helps to explain the very high proportion for the whole carers' group. But of the carers living with another adult, *a full 37 per cent live in households where nobody is earning an income.*

It is also noticeable that this group is not dominated by teenage parents. Almost 9 per cent of all 24 year olds are marginal carers, compared with just 2 per cent of all eighteen year olds.

This group is also relatively static. As Figure 12 shows, three months before the main survey, 96 per cent were off-register and just 4 per cent were in employment. Three months after the main survey, 7 per cent had entered employment and 2 per cent were unemployed and claiming unemployment benefits. The vast majority, 87 per cent, were still off-register. The relative immobility of this group is not surprising, given that two-thirds say they do not want to work because of caring duties. Lone parents in this group may be claiming benefits other than Jobseeker's Allowance: they are not all out of touch with the benefits system in the same way that other groups are, but their other characteristics suggest a high degree of isolation and marginalisation. A third of marginal carers say that they would like to work but are not looking (Fig.11).

The hidden unemployed

The 125,000 'hidden unemployed' are eighteen to 24 year olds who are ILO unemployed – actively seeking and available for work – but who say that they are not claiming benefits. The size of the group may be an overestimate because the Labour Force Survey is known to undercount the numbers claiming Jobseeker's Allowance. However, this will not account for all, or even the majority, of the 'hidden unemployed.' Young people may fall into this category for a variety of reasons: some, particularly women, will be ineligible for Jobseeker's Allowance because they have a partner who is unemployed, or conversely, they have a working partner. Nearly a quarter of the group live with a workless partner or parent. Others may choose not to claim benefits due to support from family, involvement in the informal economy or because they expect to take up a job shortly.

Their profile is very different from the marginal mothers: 55 per cent are male (Fig.4) and they are more likely to be young. Nineteen per cent are aged eighteen, compared to 11 per cent who are 24. Fourteen per cent come from ethnic minorities (Fig.5). The most significant difference from other eighteen to 24 year old groups is that nearly half of them are still living with parents (Fig.9). This is more than all other off-register groups apart from marginal learners, but still less than the average for the whole age group. Forty per cent of the total group live in workless households (Fig.8) as do 23 per cent of those who live with other adults. Again, the hidden unemployed often live with parents or partners out of work.

Compared with other off-register groups, the hidden unemployed are more mobile, have more recent experience of work and have slightly better qualification profiles. When surveyed three months earlier, 22 per cent were in work, 7 per cent were in education and a further 7 per cent were claiming unemployment-related benefits (Fig.12). However, this still leaves 54 per cent off-register for at least three months before the survey. Three months later, 26 per cent were employed and 32 per cent were claiming unemployment benefits, leaving 42 per cent still off-register. Although this group is less likely to remain hidden for long periods, it is significant that three-quarters remain not in work, training or education three months on.

The story for this group seems to be a form of fluctuating marginalisation. Slightly qualified, they want work but have low employability and are unlikely to find secure or long-term employment. Many are still dependent on their parents, which may make it a bit easier to survive on the variable income associated with not being on benefits. Over a quarter have no qualifications and another quarter have no qualifications at GCSE or above.

Compounding low educational achievement is lack of recent work experience. Twenty-six per cent say they have never had a job and a further 33 per cent have not worked in the past year. The evidence suggests that this group should therefore be primary targets for the New Deal but that many of them may not qualify because of their movement on and off the unemployment registers. It may well be that they are also active in the informal economy and that this partly explains their unwillingness to sign on. They provide perhaps the clearest illustration of the fact that many people do not move straight from work to claiming unemployment again: there are statuses in between, which can hide them from the count.

Marginal learners

Most of the off-register group consists of young people completely out of work, training and education. However, 32,000 – 6 per cent of the total – are not in work or looking for work but are studying part time. Some live in households with children and may be combining their studies with caring responsibilities, but from the survey we cannot tell how many. The statistical picture of this group should be treated with more care than for the other groups because of the small numbers involved.

Marginal learners are predominantly young and female, with a high concentration of non-white people. Sixty-three per cent are women (Fig.4) and 56 per cent of the group are aged eighteen or nineteen. As Figure 5 shows, ethnic minorities make up 22 per cent of the total – significantly higher than any other off-register group. Almost 63 per cent of marginal learners live with their parents (Fig.9), reflected in the fact that 59 per cent live in families with three adults, most of whom also have children (Fig.10). But although part-time students will almost certainly be receiving some support from parents or partners, they are also likely to come from workless households. Of those living with another adult, 32 per cent are in workless households.

Marginal learners are much more likely to have some qualifications: only 6 per cent have none. However, as Figure 6 shows, a quarter have no qualifications at GCSE level or above. Forty-one per cent have never worked and a similar proportion have not worked in the past year (Fig.7). Only a quarter say that they would like work but are not looking (Fig.11). Therefore, it is unsurprising that the group appear relatively static, with 54 per cent off-register before the main survey and around three-quarters still off-register three months after the main survey (Fig.12). Given the higher likelihood of non-completion among part-time students in sixteen to nineteen provision, many of this group may well be hovering on the edge of complete marginalisation.

The missing

Thirteen per cent of the off-register group – a full 65,000 people – are completely missing: they are not in work, education or training, they are not claiming unemployment benefits, they are not inactive because of caring duties, and they are not long-term sick or disabled. Two-thirds are women (Fig.4) and 15 per cent come from ethnic minorities (Fig.5). As Figure 6 shows, 28 per cent have no qualifications and a third have no qualifications at GCSE or above. Thirty-seven per cent say they have never worked and 45 per cent have not worked in the past year (Fig.7). Forty per cent say that they want work even though they are not looking (Fig.11).

The missing are less likely to live with their parents. As Figure 9 shows, 60 per cent live either alone or with friends or partners. A third of those not living with parents live in council or housing association housing and over half are in private rented housing. A small proportion, 13 per cent, live in owner-occupied housing.

Unlike the other off-register groups, many of the 'missing' do not live in households with children (Fig.10). Seventeen per cent live alone and 40 per cent live in two- or three-adult families with no children. Nearly a third live in households of two or three adults and children, and 11 per cent live in one parent households. The most striking feature of this group is that they are the most likely to live with other workless people. *Of those living with another adult, 43 per cent live in workless households.* If we include single parents and those living alone, we see that 59 per cent are living in households where no person is in work (Fig.8).

The missing are relatively static, although less so than other off-register groups (Fig.12). Three months before the main survey, 19 per cent were employed, 10 per cent were in full-time education and over 2 per cent were claiming unemployment benefits. The majority, 69 per cent, however, were off-register. When surveyed three months after the main survey, a similar proportion, 67 per cent, were still off-register. However, of the third who left off-register status, most had moved on to another marginal activity: only 9 per cent were working, while 24 per cent were unemployed and claiming benefits.

This group are further from labour market activity than the hidden unemployed. The relatively high proportion who say that they want to work but are not looking suggests that this group is discouraged, and the high likelihood of living with other workless adults seems to suggest that they are very much distanced from the labour market.

Status zero

The situation of sixteen and seventeen year olds not in education, training or work has provoked growing concern in recent years. Dwindling job opportunities for low-skilled school leavers, combined with the withdrawal of benefits for sixteen and seventeen year olds seeking work and replacement with a training guarantee, seem to have contributed to a growth in the numbers completely out of the system.

In this section, we try to find out how many there are and take a closer look at their profile and experience. We draw on a range of sources, including local studies, the Labour Force Survey, Careers Service Activity Surveys and the Youth Cohort Survey.

The scale of status zero has been particularly highlighted by local studies in Mid and South Glamorgan, which revealed that the problem affected between 16 and 23 per cent of sixteen and seventeen year olds at any one time. This is much larger than the 6.5 per cent suggested by the Careers Service, which is supposed to collect comprehensive data on school leavers' destinations. The

Careers Service destinations surveys, however, while presenting a useful picture of the majority of young people, shed little light on the status of the most marginalised. Around 8 per cent of the whole age group and 5 per cent of young people in year 11 are not on careers registers in the first place. Of those who are, Careers Services fail to contact 7 per cent. In all, the national Careers Service Activity Survey misses 9 per cent of year 11 students and nearly 15 per cent of the age group.

To gain a clearer picture of status zero across the UK, we re-analysed LFS data. This suggests that around one in ten sixteen and seventeen year olds are not in work, full-time education or training. If we exclude the small number of part-time students, the status zero figure is 8.2 per cent. This figure is slightly higher than the Department for Education and Employment's current estimate of 7.6 per cent, which is derived by integrating education, training records and information from the Labour Force Survey. Careers Service data shows substantial local variations: in Salford and Tameside, almost 11 per cent are known to be status zero and 12 per cent go to unknown destinations. In Shropshire, just 3 per cent are status zero and about 5 per cent go to unknown destinations.

As with all household surveys, our figure will under-represent the most marginalised and mobile young people and the true figure is likely to be higher. Although the exact figure is impossible to calculate, there is clearly a significant minority losing their place in the institutional framework. What do we know about them?

The profile of the status zero group: youth at risk
Nearly half of those in status zero have no qualifications and only 37 per cent have GCSEs or above. The Mid Glamorgan study found a similar proportion with no GCSEs and a third who had no GCSEs at grades A to C. According to the Youth Cohort Survey, 28 per cent of young people with no qualifications are not in work, training or education at sixteen and a third are in this position at eighteen. For those with better qualifications, the passage is far less risky. Fifteen per cent of young people with five GCSEs below grade C are not in education, training or work at eighteen. The figure for those with five GCSEs at grade C or above is just 3 per cent.

Low educational attainment is often associated with other problems such as truancy, school exclusion, early parenthood or being in care. Around three-quarters of young people who have been in care get no qualifications, and 60 per cent of teenage mothers have no qualifications by their early twenties. Given their education profile, these young people are likely to feature in the status zero group. The Youth Cohort Survey shows that 23 per cent of the off-

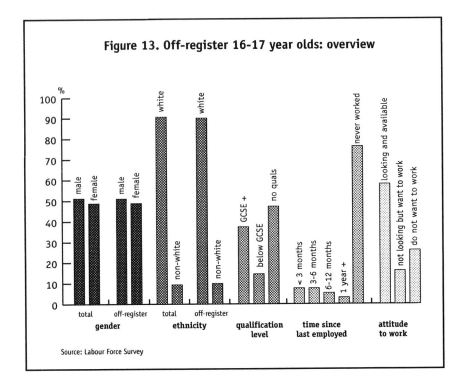

Figure 13. Off-register 16-17 year olds: overview

Source: Labour Force Survey

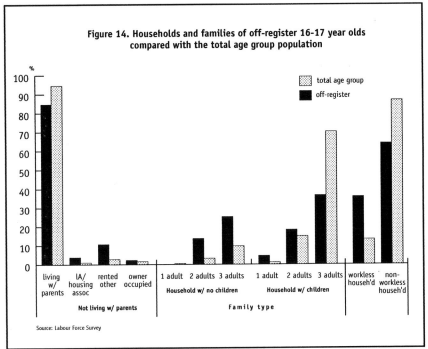

Figure 14. Households and families of off-register 16-17 year olds compared with the total age group population

Source: Labour Force Survey

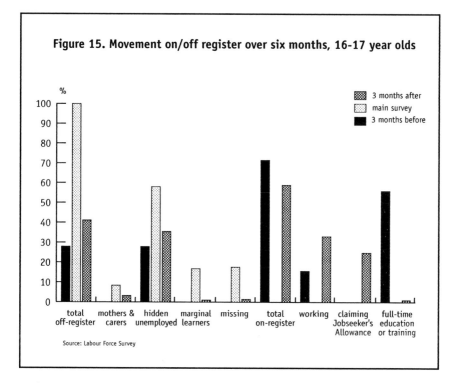

Figure 15. Movement on/off register over six months, 16-17 year olds

Legend:
- 3 months after
- main survey
- 3 months before

Categories: total off-register, mothers & carers, hidden unemployed, marginal learners, missing, total on-register, working, claiming Jobseeker's Allowance, full-time education or training

Source: Labour Force Survey

register group persistently truanted, compared with 6 per cent of those on government-supported training. One in three of persistent truants end up outside education, employment or training at sixteen, compared with just 3 per cent of non-truants.

Certain ethnic minorities are more likely to appear. According to Careers Service data, 19 per cent of 'black African' young people and 'black other' are either status zero or in unknown destinations, compared with just 7 per cent of Indians and Chinese. Thirteen per cent of white young people are in unknown destinations or status zero.

Over three-quarters of the group say that they have never worked, with just 15 per cent having worked in the past six months. This is despite the fact that 58 per cent are seeking and available for work, much higher than among eighteen to 24 year olds. A further 16 per cent want to work but are not looking and 26 per cent do not want to work. Of these last two groups, 17 per cent are not looking because they are part-time students, 8 per cent have caring duties and 18 per cent say they have 'other' reasons for not seeking work.

There are some important differences between the sixteen to seventeen year old and eighteen to 24 year old groups. Eighty-five per cent live with their parents, compared to 28 per cent of eighteen to 24 year olds. Thirty per cent of those in status zero who are living with another adult live in workless households. Of even more concern are the 20,000 young people who have left home early and are living away from parents. Some of this group may include the 8,000 young people who leave care each year. Work from the Youth Cohort Survey shows that 27 per cent of sixteen year olds living with neither parent were in status zero and 40 per cent were not in education or training. Those not living with parents seem to be at serious risk.

The second important difference is gender balance. Where other off-register groups contain disproportionate numbers of females, the gender balance for the status zero group is more even: 51 per cent are male. The figures from South Glamorgan TEC and from the Careers Service suggest around 55 per cent are male. The Mid Glamorgan study reveals a more complex gender dynamic. Men were more likely to be in status zero for between six and nineteen months, while women were slightly more likely to have stayed on at school and then subsequently to have dropped out.

Status zero: dynamics

Off-register sixteen to seventeen year olds are much more mobile than the older groups. Seventy-two per cent were not off-register three months before the main survey. Most were in school or other full-time education or training. Only 16 per cent were in work.

Once off-register, however, most fail to move on to a positive activity. Two-thirds are still not in work, training or education, with a quarter now claiming unemployment-related benefits, because they have either turned eighteen or managed to prove severe hardship. A third have moved into work. The most common occupational destination for off-register sixteen to 24 year olds was personal and protective services, which accounted for 40 per cent of all employment. This sector includes jobs in catering, security, domestic work and childcare, many of which may provide temporary income but little opportunity to progress. The Youth Cohort Survey shows that one in five young people who were in work at sixteen were out of work, training or education at eighteen, and one in ten were on government-supported training.

Around one in ten sixteen and seventeen year olds were in status zero at the moment of the survey. But how many will experience it at some point? The Mid Glamorgan study found that only 44 per cent of all young people were in continuous education throughout the two years after leaving school. Of the remainder, only one in ten managed to avoid being off-register during the next two years – either through sustained work or training. Around half the age group therefore experienced status zero at some point. Although 90 per cent of those not in education continuously for two years had some experience of status zero, 38 per cent experienced it for between six and nineteen months, and almost 16 per cent for twenty months or longer. Of the group that spent between six and nineteen months off-register, 40 per cent did so in one spell, a third did so in two spells and a quarter did so in three or more spells. This illustrates that within the off-register group there are both young people who stay relatively static and others who cycle between status zero and other activities. Perhaps of most concern is the core group that remains outside provision for long spells. The Youth Cohort Survey shows that 3 per cent of young people were not in education, training or employment at sixteen, seventeen or eighteen. Over half of those not in education, training or employment at sixteen were in the same position at seventeen and a third of those still remained there at eighteen.

Combinations of risk

A number of factors clearly increases the risk of being off-register, including leaving school with no qualifications and living in a workless household. However, it is striking how the *combination* of different factors produced acute risk. For instance, 29 per cent of young eighteen to 24 year olds with no qualifications are off-register as are 31 per cent of those living in workless households. However, 58 per cent of young people who both have no qualifications and live in workless households are off-register. Combining household and family type, we find that, while the overall risk of being off-register among those living in workless households is 31 per cent, and among those living away from parents in local authority housing it is 41 per cent, the risk among those living away from parents in local authority housing *and* living in a workless household is 64 per cent.

Similarly, 19 per cent of eighteen to 24 year olds living in households with children are off-register, as are 31 per cent of those living in workless households. But of those living in workless households *with* children, 58 per cent are off-register. Combinations and clusters of risk are of crucial importance to understanding the problem and its possible solutions.

The costs and implications of the off-register problem

These five groups of sixteen to 24 year olds – mothers, the hidden unemployed, the marginal learners, the missing and status zero sixteen to seventeen year olds – represent a major challenge to society. Their situation means that they are detached from the primary routes to fulfilment and independence in adulthood. The fact that they are not claiming unemployment benefits means that

Figure 16. The off-register groups: labour market prospects and status

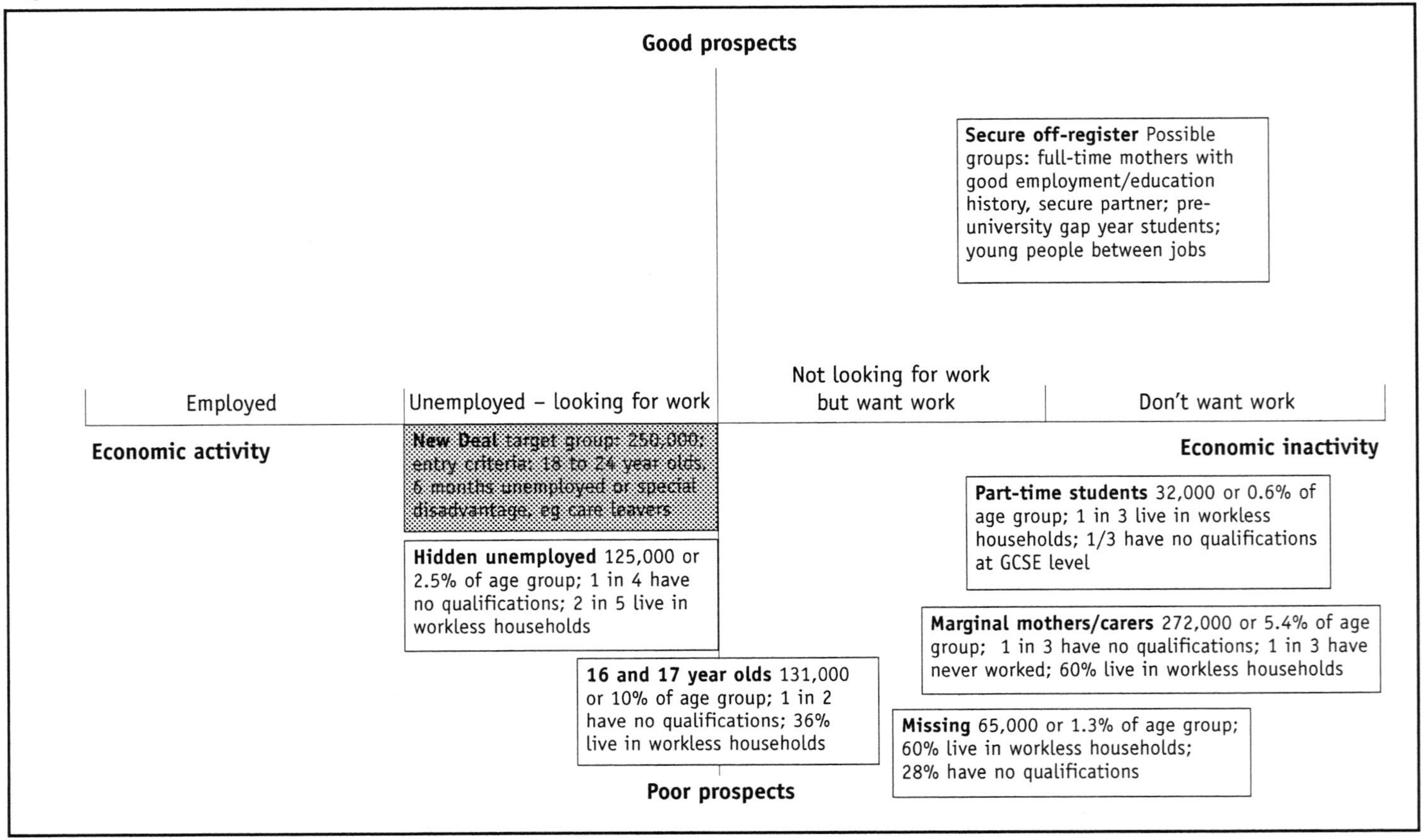

Good prospects

Economic activity

| Employed | Unemployed – looking for work | Not looking for work but want work | Don't want work |

Secure off-register Possible groups: full-time mothers with good employment/education history, secure partner; pre-university gap year students; young people between jobs

Economic inactivity

New Deal target group 250,000 entry criteria: 18 to 24 year olds 6 months unemployed or special disadvantage, eg care leavers

Hidden unemployed 125,000 or 2.5% of age group; 1 in 4 have no qualifications; 2 in 5 live in workless households

16 and 17 year olds 131,000 or 10% of age group; 1 in 2 have no qualifications; 36% live in workless households

Part-time students 32,000 or 0.6% of age group; 1 in 3 live in workless households; 1/3 have no qualifications at GCSE level

Marginal mothers/carers 272,000 or 5.4% of age group; 1 in 3 have no qualifications; 1 in 3 have never worked; 60% live in workless households

Missing 65,000 or 1.3% of age group; 60% live in workless households; 28% have no qualifications

Poor prospects

they do not even show up in the statistics conventionally used to measure non-participation. Among the mothers and carers group it is likely that many are claiming other benefits, such as income support. This means that they are not as invisible as the other sub-groups. But their profile shows that many of them are as marginalised as those who do not appear on any benefit register.

This invisibility is one reason why the problem has not being fully recognised until now. Young people who do not show up in official statistics have often been conveniently ignored. Even if they do cause concern, it is very difficult to track and trace them. Another reason is that this status could be one which people choose. The economists' assumption would be that people will always seek to maximise their income by claiming benefits if they can. If people choose to have children, they should also take responsibility for the implications. Similarly, if people choose not to take part in education or training, who can make them after they pass the school leaving age? Why should anybody bother to try?

The first reason is that this assumption of straightforward choice is mistaken. More than half of this group of young people want to work and a third are actively seeking jobs, despite their marginal status. Many others will have been discouraged by repeated negative experience of the labour market, education institutions and training programmes. Direct evidence from the consultation which ran alongside this research project – The Real Deal – shows that many young people who have experienced this degree of marginalisation are disillusioned about their prospects of getting anywhere.[32] It also shows that life in the low-skill labour market is disjointed and exploitative, with many recounting stories of underpayment, unpredictability and unfairness by employers. The most consistent theme to emerge from the Real Deal consultation was that the aspirations of these young people, despite the severity of their experiences, are no different from most other people's: they want jobs, homes, families and positive relationships. They do not want to be seen as problems to society but to be recognised for their potential to contribute and to create solutions.

The second reason is that the off-register group as a whole displays characteristics that are markers of serious exclusion: they are far more likely to have no or few qualifications, to live in or come from workless households and to have little or no past experience of work. Whatever the specific causes of their situation, they are in grave danger of being excluded from participation in mainstream society. Analysis of the British Household Panel Study shows that being out of work and having low educational attainment also mean a greater likelihood of social isolation, troubled relationships and low participation in civic, cultural or recreational life.[33]

The third reason is that the experience of marginal status at this formative stage of early adulthood is deeply damaging to long-term life chances. Although detailed longitudinal evidence is still relatively scarce, there is enough to show that it is the *experience*, as well as background factors such as childhood poverty and lack of qualifications, which contributes to long-term marginalisation.

Analysis of the JUVOS database, which records claims for unemployment benefit, shows that there is a strong correlation between unemployment among nineteen to twenty year olds and the likelihood of unemployment four years later. Both the length of time for which they were claiming and the number of claims within a two-year period are strongly associated with the likelihood of claiming again later on (Figs. 17 and 18). While 17 per cent of those who claimed once during 1992–93 were claimants four years later, among those who claimed twice in 1992–93 the figure rises to 32 per cent and for those who claimed four times the figure is 62 per cent.

Analysis by Paul Gregg of the National Child Development Survey shows a similar picture. While young people with no experience of unemployment between sixteen and 23 were unemployed for just 1.6 per cent of the following ten years, those unemployed for six to twelve months in this early period were unemployed for almost 11 per cent of the time between the ages of 23 and 33. For those unemployed for more than a year between sixteen and 23, the figure rises to almost 23 per cent. All of these groups spent an even longer period non-employed, that is, not working and not registered as unemployed, than they spent registered unemployed. Even more important than the simple increase in the likelihood of unemployment is the fact that, when other variables which influence the chances of unemployment – education, geographical region, ability and social background – are controlled for, the same pattern still emerges. As the author puts it,

about two-thirds of the raw correlation between higher early unemployment and higher late unemployment is down to the unemployment itself, and one-third because of area or individual variation.[34]

Similar studies in the United States and Sweden have shown that failure to make an early transition to permanent work or to full-time study is associated with long-term risks of marginalisation, helping to trap people in a cycle of unemployment, part-time work and government schemes.[35]

Alongside the long-term cost to individuals and their families, there is a wider cost to society and the state. Although most of this group are not costing

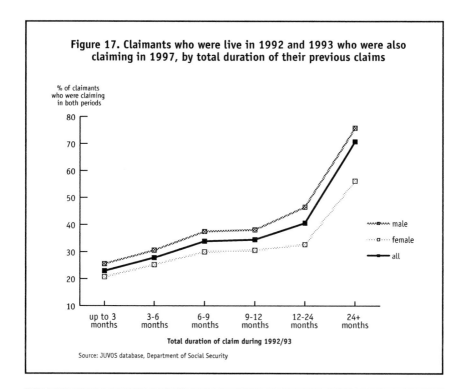

Figure 17. Claimants who were live in 1992 and 1993 who were also claiming in 1997, by total duration of their previous claims

% of claimants who were claiming in both periods

Total duration of claim during 1992/93

Source: JUVOS database, Department of Social Security

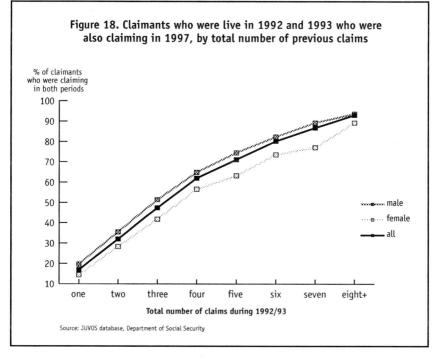

Figure 18. Claimants who were live in 1992 and 1993 who were also claiming in 1997, by total number of previous claims

% of claimants who were claiming in both periods

Total number of claims during 1992/93

Source: JUVOS database, Department of Social Security

the taxpayer directly through unemployment benefits, given that nearly half the group live in workless households, a proportion will be claiming other benefits including housing benefit, income support and lone parent benefits. Since this group is so static, they are likely to claim benefits over a long period. Individuals with no qualifications are also much more likely to start claiming sickness and disability benefits. In 1997, three-quarters of economically inactive men with no qualifications were inactive due to sickness. The association of marginal and unemployed status with poor mental and physical health, crime, family trauma and poverty means that the likely cost of income maintenance and other public services over a lifetime are huge. If we think not just of the future costs of the off-register group but of the previous costs of some young people who end up off-register, the cost becomes even more staggering. Given the profile of the group, and what we know about the factors which lead to leaving home and school early, poor qualifications and marginal employment status, particular groups are likely to be over-represented. These include young people with experience of care, truancy, school exclusion and crime. As testified by some young people in the Real Deal consultation, many will have come into contact with a wide range of public service agencies: education welfare officers, police and courts, social services and so on. Because the cost of these services is not aggregated horizontally around the individuals and groups who use them most, it is impossible to put a figure on them. But for many, it is vast and does not contribute to positive long-term progression.

Added to this is the opportunity cost of *lost contribution*. Given that large numbers are likely to be inactive or unemployed later in life, they will fail to contribute to the economy and to tax revenues. Even if just 50,000 out of the 624,000 off-register moved into low-paid work, their contribution through direct and indirect taxes would be considerable. By way of example, if these 50,000 people contributed £2,000 in income, national insurance and consumption taxes over the course of a year, they would contribute £100 million in all. If 250,000 off-register young people moved into work and contributed a similar amount, they would generate £1 billion pounds over the course of two years. These sums do not take into account any benefit savings and are a low estimate of potential tax contributions. The potential savings over time are immense even if relatively small numbers are moved into work. The potential to contribute is not just measured financially. Marginalisation of this kind also blunts people's capacity to contribute as parents, citizens and community members and affects the quality of collective life as a result.

Why has this problem passed us by?

Increasing participation by women in the labour force has helped to mask the decline in economic activity among key groups.[36] Frequent changes in the official definition of unemployment (it was changed more than 40 times between 1979 and 1997, always in ways which reduced the total number) have meant a growing disparity between the numbers counted as unemployed and the numbers genuinely out of work. Rising educational attainment among the majority of young people has helped to obscure the growing risks facing the persistent minority who leave the system with few or no qualifications. The fact that many young people successfully combine work in temporary, insecure and part-time jobs with educational careers which will give them greater security later on has obscured the fact that those for whom insecure work is the only form of engagement are less likely to be progressing anywhere. The fact that marriage and stable family structure are far less common has helped to hide the reality that those most at risk of economic marginalisation are also least likely to rely on wide social networks and strong relationships. In an environment characterised by growing choice, flexibility and diversity, we have failed to recognise that lack of structure and coherence in many young people's experience makes it harder for them to progress to a level of independence where they can make real choices about their lives.

Policy implications

The UK government has signalled its determination to encourage participation through work and learning and to reduce and prevent social exclusion in the long term. If it is going to succeed, it must address the off-register problem wholeheartedly. This depends partly on creating a framework for long-term prevention that begins with families and young children. Several policies, including the Working Families Tax Credit, the expansion of childcare and the Sure Start programme, and strategies to raise literacy and numeracy among primary school children, are already contributing to this goal. But it also means a sustained campaign to engage with and support those young people who are already on the margins: those whose attachment to mainstream forms of participation is currently too weak to ensure that they can become independent, active contributors to society. Alongside measures targeted specifically at those most at risk, this will involve long-term reform of the whole framework of education, training and social support.

The evidence and analysis we have presented in this chapter have several major implications for policy. In particular, they point to the need for:

- better information about the status, progress and activities of young people, both before and after they leave compulsory education
- more effective tools for managing knowledge and acting on indications of risk, within the overall framework of provision
- active targeting and engagement of those young people on the edges of the mainstream system
- creation of clear, coherent pathways to secure, independent adult status at every level of attainment; these pathways must address the *combinations* of activities and resources which contribute to positive long-term development
- a framework of entitlement that reflects the real life circumstances and activities of young people most at risk
- effective support for the transition between different forms of activity, including the transition from school to post-compulsory learning and transitions in and out of work
- effective forms of communication with young people: in basic terms, staying in touch
- measures to prevent the isolation and marginalisation of young parents, especially single mothers.

The rest of the report addresses the questions of whether and how these challenges can be met. It draws on evidence from case studies of local projects and programmes, interviews and consultation with young people, evaluation studies and good practice from other countries. The evidence and practice we have found support the view that it is possible to make an impact on the problem of off-register youth. We are not talking about a 'lost generation'. It is not determined in advance that young people who find themselves in this situation will never find a way into safe, productive, fulfilling, adult lives.

What can be done?

The problems faced by young people have, of course, not gone unnoticed. As governments have recognised education as a growing priority and the social economic and community problems described above have become increasingly expensive and visible, there has been a wide range of responses. In the UK, initiatives to tackle drugs, crime, homelessness, unemployment and school standards have been announced. Some, like the Rough Sleeper's Initiative, have undoubtedly had some impact on single problems faced by at-risk young people. Despite the fact that cash benefits have become harder to access, real spending on most services for young people has increased, especially in core areas like schools.

The resources available, both financial and more broadly, are probably greater than ever before. The current UK government has made young people one of its highest social priorities, with a range of initiatives to match. Numerical targets are being used to an unprecedented extent: 250,000 off benefits and into work, increases in numeracy and literacy standards for eleven year olds, truancy and school exclusions to be cut by a third over five years.

The danger, though, is that the new focus on individual problems may exacerbate the failures created by the *fragmentation* and increasing *complexity* of public service delivery, a process which has been going on for at least fifteen years in the UK. In order to address marginalisation effectively, we must understand how the framework of services and supports – the public service infrastructure – has contributed to some young people's disengagement from the mainstream.

Tackling the problem is not just a question of identifying it as a priority or of spending more money on it. In many of the projects we have visited, experienced and innovative practitioners have told us that 'more resources is not necessarily the answer'. Throwing public money at the problem without proper understanding of its causes or possible solutions is a recipe for failure and disillusionment. There is a strong case for public investment in prevention through re-engagement, but we must ensure that it will yield a return. This depends on better understanding of five core elements:

- the failure of the *public service framework*
- how to identify and operationalise *risk*
- the range of *opportunities and resources* which could support positive progression
- creating and managing *knowledge that works*
- effective *work with young people.*

The first three of these are covered in this chapter. Chapter four then addresses the last two by examining what works in practice.

The failure of the public service framework

Overall, two features characterise the changes which have taken place in the public service framework over the last fifteen years. First, we have seen a *sharper focus* on the objectives and performance of individual services and agencies: school league tables and inspection, Employment Service performance targets, police performance indicators based on arrest rates, and so on. In parallel, there has been a loosening of the overall infrastructure through a combination of privatisation, devolution of management and introduction of market-based funding and regulatory regimes. Examples of this include local management of schools, privatisation of the Careers Service, the creation of training and enterprise councils, the purchaser-provider split in local government, the growth of voluntary sector contracting and competition between education providers for sixteen to nineteen year olds.

Despite the growth of audit, inspection and performance indicators, this combination has made it more difficult for different agencies to work *in concert* to achieve shared objectives and common outcomes. Perhaps the clearest example is the correlation between the introduction of school league tables in the early 1990s with a massive rise in permanent school exclusions. Another is that privatised Careers Service companies, because of commercial interest, have less incentive to share data on the destinations of young people with local authorities and other agencies.

In particular, the framework of institutions and agencies for young people after sixteen can be almost impossibly fragmented and incoherent. Finding your way through the range of labour market, education, social support, benefit, criminal justice, health and other agencies, which come from the private, public and voluntary sectors, can become a Kafka-esque experience. Very often

the onus is on the young person to make sense of it all. The patchwork c
tlements and rules, the range of locations from which they are available
the tangled complexity of information about services and support all m,
them more difficult for young people to access.

Sixteen is the point at which the direction of early adult life should be begin
ning to take shape. As we have seen, the late teens and early twenties are a more
influential *formative stage* than a generation ago, because of the investment in
knowledge, skills and social capital needed to thrive in contemporary society.
The range of available support therefore ought to be organised around the
needs and preferences of the citizen. But partly because the transitions to adulthood during this phase have become more complex and protracted, the range
of activities, supports and pathways has increased. This means that the scope
for personalisation and creativity is greater, but only if young people have the
support, security and life skills needed to adapt resources and opportunities to
their own needs. One example of this is the growing number who take a year
off between school and university, an experience which can enhance skills and
broaden horizons, contributing to overall development rather than disrupting
the transition.

However, for young people who are experiencing difficulties and for whom
sustained and valuable family support is not forthcoming, the maze of institutions, options and possible opportunities does little to protect them from the
risks which also appear. The looseness of the structures through which they
pass becomes a problem, rather than a chance to make meaningful choices.

For young people who drift out of contact with the institutional framework
– those who truant or are excluded from school, those who leave with few
qualifications and do not find their way into post-sixteen education, those who
leave care without systematic follow-up support (those who are less likely to
show up on official registers) – this problem becomes acute.

Not only are they already more at risk, they are also less likely to be in regular contact with the agencies responsible for different aspects of their well-
being. When they pass sixteen, the problem worsens considerably. Education
and training providers, whose performance and funding levels are often determined by *outputs* – qualifications and courses completed – have had little
incentive to take on those with lower chances of success. Other provision
remains fragmented: the Careers Service is required to follow up young people
with destinations surveys and offers of support, but have typically done so in
limited ways, such as letters and occasional phone calls. There is a growing disparity between the number of fifteen year olds on school rolls and the estimated total population, suggesting that more are leaking out of the institu-

school leaving age. Records of attendance and
.ed on in any detail from one education or training
_yond the post-sixteen divide, especially where there is
.iich the information can be passed on straight away.
.nd Housing Benefit are only available to the small minority
.eventeen year olds who qualify for severe hardship. These illus-
.w how making sustained progress over time, and gaining access to
.ort that you need, have become dependent on the individual, rather
.he state. Positive forms of support: guidance, education, income main-
.iance, depend largely on being persistent, negotiating with different agencies, and pulling resources together.

Vulnerable young people are more likely to come into contact with services
dealing with acute *problems,* such as crime, health or emergency homelessness
services. Although there are examples of good practice, the transition from acute
and emergency case management through to continued support and positive
progression is rare and difficult to achieve. Social Services departments have
become more likely to concentrate their hard-pressed budgets and staff on
acute child protection cases rather than the family support and mediation
more likely to be needed by adolescents. Other agencies dealing with acute
problems are not always funded to provide longer term support, and often have
to pass on provider responsibility to statutory agencies such as housing departments and Social Services, with negative consequences. For example, a high proportion of homeless young people rehoused by voluntary agencies find themselves back on the streets. Yet it is very difficult for such agencies to prove that
their clients qualify for Housing Benefit, ironically because they often lack institutional records and proof of identity.

What of the voluntary and community sectors? Specific organisations and
partnerships are excelling in particular areas of practice, making a positive
impact with limited resources, but the structure of their contracts and the difficulty of dealing with large-scale bureaucratic infrastructures often limits the
scope for sustained support. Cultures of cooperation and collaboration are
often highly limited. The voluntary youth sector, which contains some beacons
of professionalism and good practice, is at odds in many areas with local
authority youth services, with relationships characterised by mutual suspicion
and antipathy. Charities that have developed core competences in specific areas
such as housing management or drugs counselling find themselves dealing
with a wide range of connected challenges, such as lack of basic skills, mental
health needs and continued family conflict.

It is important to avoid over-generalisation and not paint the quality of services with too broad a brush. Many young people pass through this stage with flying colours. Many more negotiate their passage well enough to get by and move on to holding down a job or keeping a family together. Many agencies, both public and voluntary, do a superb job and make a real difference, as we will see in the next section. But part of the problem is that making a difference to a single dimension in isolation from the wider context is often not enough to support the progression of the whole person. The focus on institutional effectiveness, individual performance indicators and outpacing the competition works against the imperative to provide the *full range* of support needed, in the right combination and at the right time.

To support this overall development, educational experience must be matched with financial and material support, leisure and recreational opportunities with interpersonal and financial literacy skills, freedom and responsibility with appropriate role models and adult guidance. For the high achievers, universities and residential colleges can provide the semi-structured social and institutional context in which to negotiate these new risks and opportunities, as long as financial and other supports are available. But for those without a linear educational career to pursue, support and opportunity are either non-existent or frustratingly disparate.

If they are to support positive transitions for all, services for young people must be organised around a new unit of integration – the life of *the young person* rather than the budgets of a government department, the productivity of an educational sector or even the structure of a specific programme like the New Deal.

This is why the challenge is not just to improve the quality and relevance of individual interventions or services but to find the right ways of *combining and connecting* these services. Otherwise, the money and effort are wasted. As Frances Ianni concluded in a comprehensive review of programmes for at-risk youth in the United States, a set of *coherent expectations* among the people and institutions in a young person's life was the most striking ingredient in the young person's successful adaptation and progress: 'We soon discovered that the harmony and accord among the institutions and what their adolescent members heard from them *in concert* was what scored the adolescent experience.'[37] To be genuinely effective, they must work in concert to produce outcomes that make sense from a personal, as well as an institutional, perspective.

Understanding risk

The story so far has highlighted a range of outcomes for young people which contribute to long-term social exclusion. We have focused on off-register status, the progressive loss of contact with education, mainstream institutions, economic activity and community membership. Various others during the transition to adulthood, from teenage parenthood to homelessness, diminish the longer-term life chances of the young people who experience them. The statistical analysis and volumes of other research show that a cluster of factors and characteristics in childhood and adolescence increase the risk of marginalisation later on.

These risks have become more concentrated on particular individuals. For example, for people born in 1958 the risk of youth unemployment was spread relatively evenly across individuals with different levels of educational basic skills. For the cohort born in 1970 with a good education record the risk of unemployment is similar to that of their predecessors, but for those with poor qualifications and low basic skills the risk is far greater.[38] Other resources are also influential, including family background, social networks and psychological factors such as self-esteem and motivation. In other words, the risk of exclusion is not random – it is concentrated on young people who, through their experiences and circumstances, lack certain material, educational, social, cultural and psychological resources. If these deficits are identified in the right ways they can contribute to *early warning systems* that help to target support towards those most in need.

But there are several problems with mapping risk. The first is that experience of a single risk factor does not automatically lead to serious social exclusion. Many young people growing up in poverty do not leave school with no qualifications or experience long-term unemployment, even though a disproportionate number do. Not all those who truant from school find themselves off-register, although again, they are more likely to. There is no simple, mechanistic way of equating individual risk factors with negative outcomes and no straightforward link between identification of risk factors and providing effective responses. The situation facing each young person is different.

The challenge is to find the right way of identifying those who are *more likely* to need specific help and support and then to create systems that can produce packages of support which are effective and appropriate for each individual.

Although individual risks do not always lead straightforwardly to specific outcomes or solutions, there is a remarkable consistency of risk factors for the range of outcomes associated with long-term social exclusion. In particular, when different risk factors *combine* in a cluster of circumstances and experiences that reinforce each other, the overall risk becomes acute.

As we have seen, social and economic change over the past two decades has produced a concentration of disadvantage which makes the combination of risk factors much more likely for young people growing up in disadvantaged circumstances. This concentration includes the clustering of low income and workless households in particular neighbourhoods, often places where educational achievement is far below the national average, and the residualisation of public housing, creating estates where the majority of residents are economically inactive, crime is high and positive opportunities for young people are severely constrained.

See Figure 19 for the factors which, on the evidence available, contribute to negative outcomes for young people.

The impact of early childhood experience on later life chances has had a strong influence on policies designed to reduce exclusion in the UK, including early years education, the Sure Start programme and the national literacy and numeracy strategies. The early years are indeed the most influential. Over a fifth of the variation in literacy and numeracy levels among adults aged 37 can be explained by circumstances and experiences in the first seven years of life.[39]

However, the period between seven and sixteen is also crucial. For instance, for women, although 22 per cent of the variation in literacy and numeracy scores at 37 is accounted for by age seven, 35 per cent can be explained by age sixteen. Added to this is the fact that while background factors make a difference, they only account for 40 per cent of the variation in basic skills among adults aged 33. The rest of the difference is determined by factors which are less predictable, such as social networks, motivation and the jobs and courses young people take up. If the right forms of support and intervention are employed, there is significant scope for improving the circumstances even of those young people who have already experienced serious disadvantage.

The distribution of risk

As we have seen, the risks that contribute to negative outcomes for young adults are not evenly distributed. It is the *interaction* of different risk factors which most often produces the greatest danger, particularly when they become mutually reinforcing. In order to target support and resources, we must be able to identify the interaction between three basic dimensions of risk.

Personal, family and household characteristics

Specific factors such as growing up in poverty, experiencing family conflict during early childhood, living in overcrowded housing and coming from particular ethnic backgrounds all increase the risk of marginalisation. They also tend to cluster together. For example, ten per cent of young children grow up in poor housing. Of the 3 per cent who *also* live in run-down areas, 65 per cent are the children of lone, non-employed or ethnic minority parents.[40]

Figure 19. Risk factors for young people

Material	Educational	Employment	Family and peer	Psychological and physical health
Poor living conditions: vandalism, general disrepair, high number of voids	Poor visual motor skills Poor early cognitive development Poor primary to secondary transition	Lack of work-related skills eg IT, interpersonal or work-specific skills	Troubled relationships between parents, between parents and children, and between siblings	Alcohol, drug or solvent abuse
Council housing in economically run-down areas	Temperamental difficulties: hyperactivity, impulsiveness and attention disorder	Self-perception of skills as poor, narrow or 'traditional'	Been in care Parental abuse, absence or neglect	Psycho-social disorders, eg anorexia, self-harm, depression
High turnover and lack of attachment	Low teacher commitment to child	Leaves school at 16 to enter employment or GST Criminal record	Harsh, cruel and inconsistent discipline	Low self-esteem, self-concern
Low family income <£150 a week	Low parental interest in child education Poor home–school relationship Poor intake and/or teaching in school	Temporary, low-paid employment Dropped out of training or education course	Parents with drug or alcohol problems, mental health problems Criminal history	
	Low attainment at school eg very low stream, poor projected grades Truancy, non-attendance Behavioural problems, eg statemented	High incidence and/or duration of unemployment or inactivity Off-register: sick, informal worker, carer	Workless households Father long-term unemployed	
	Poor basic reading and numeracy skills Fixed term/permanent exclusion		Family break-up and reconstitution Lone parent	
			Peer group involved in anti-social behaviour: crime, bullying, drug and alcohol use, truancy etc	

Another illustration of the clustering of risk is the strong link between crim truancy and exclusion from school: 30 per cent of daytime burglaries are committed by ten to sixteen year olds.[41] School exclusions are strongly linked to family problems and violence in the home: 20 per cent of permanently excluded pupils are also on social services registers.[42] A recent survey found that two-fifths of young people excluded from school had been involved in violent arguments in the home.[43] A recent study of the risk of youth homelessness revealed that both being excluded from school and living with a step-parent increases the risk of homelessness independently, but when both these factors are present in an individual, the risk of homelessness increases significantly.[44]

Local mapping exercises often reveal that although young people may appear on one particular agency's records, their problems have many dimensions. In Milton Keynes, for example, a fifth of the children on the child protection register are known to have parents suffering from either mental health problems, learning difficulties or substance abuse.[45] The same mapping exercise revealed clear correlations between the numbers of free school meals and the number of pupils with statements of special educational needs, the numbers of permanent and fixed-term exclusions, truancy and juvenile crime rates, and the number of pupils in care.

Geographical area

By almost any measure, deprivation and disadvantage are concentrated in specific areas. Perhaps the most striking examples are the public housing estates characterised by high crime, unemployment, poor literacy and high mortality.[46] These concentrations of disadvantage are relatively static. Of the most deprived ten areas in the 1998 Index of Local Deprivation, eight were in the worst ten in 1991. Of the worst 50 in 1996–98, no fewer than 46 were in the worst 50 in 1991.

There are substantial regional variations in patterns of risk. Fifty per cent of pupils in the South-east, Scotland and Northern Ireland obtain five or more GCSEs above grade C, compared to 38 per cent of pupils in the North-east and Merseyside. The disparities are far larger if we compare schools or estates within in a particular area. One study found that in secondary schools serving 'difficult to let' estates, one in four children gain no GCSEs compared to a national average of one in twenty and truancy rates are four times the national average. The disparities between schools in a particular area are often staggering. In one state school in Leeds, 67 per cent of fifteen year olds achieved high grade GCSEs in 1997 compared with just 3 per cent in another school in the same city. In the top ten schools, 57 per cent achieved high grade GCSEs, while in the bottom ten, the average was less than 13 per cent. Part of the explanation

s is the differing intakes of the various schools. In the low-
, three-quarters of pupils are from households in receipt
he highest the figure is less than 3 per cent.

e clearly concentrated in particular areas, there is also
dispersion. One government study identifying young people on
low incomes who were living with a workless single mother showed that
although 230,000 were in 'deprived' areas, 390,000 were located in other areas.
Although young children living in deprived areas were much more likely to be
classified as 'at risk' – one in four compared with one in ten – a strategy targeted exclusively at deprived areas would miss out more than three-fifths of all
at-risk children.[47]

Although risk can be identified to some extent by targeting at-risk neighbourhoods, individuals at risk are also dispersed. Creating effective early warning systems requires a combination of geographical, individual, family and
household information.

Life stages and transitions

Risk is also reduced or increased by the timing of *key life events*. Younger people are generally more at risk of job displacement. Those who leave home and
school early are more at risk of unemployment and homelessness. Teenage
mothers are more likely to be unemployed and poor as adults.

In general, life events such as changing jobs, leaving education and moving
home are risky because they involve stress and uncertainty. These are transitions that every young person goes through; in themselves, they are not
grounds for targeting or undue concern. The danger, again, lies in their conjunction with other factors: when stressful changes, such as leaving care and
education, take place simultaneously, when family and household circumstances such as overcrowding or domestic violence help to trigger a life stage,
or when an event such as childbirth interrupts another process of progression
such as education.

The risks caused by the timing of life events imply two priorities for policy.
First, we should look at reducing the number of transitions that have to be
made *simultaneously* by young people already at risk. Second, we should pay
more attention to the processes of *preparation* and *follow-through* that accompany such changes.

Dynamics of risks: vicious cycles

Although we know that clusters of risk factors increase the likelihood of negative outcomes, the actual processes of interaction are far more difficult to

understand. The causes and effects are too detailed, and too individualised, to draw out of any but the most detailed observation.

But effective use of risk indicators does not necessarily depend on the academic ideal of identifying the true cause–effect relationship. Risk indicators should primarily be used to identify the need for support, rather than automatically to trigger a particular intervention. In policy terms, the cause–effect question is better directed at the relationship between interventions and outcomes.

The key point about the interaction of risk factors is that they become mutually reinforcing, creating *vicious cycles*. Childhood poverty increases the risk of poor qualifications, which in turn increases the risk of unemployment, leading to a greater risk of poverty. Lack of self-esteem, problematic family interactions, poverty and poor school performance are known to be interconnected and to mutually reinforce each other.[48] Conversely, self-confidence both encourages and is boosted by success in education. Drug and alcohol abuse is known to be a cause and effect of homelessness. Similarly, there is a well-known link between drug taking and crime, and between school problems such as truancy or exclusion and youth offending. The mutual reinforcement of these risk factors creates spirals which can lead to deeper marginalisation.

Again, the implication for policy is straightforward: the goal must be to create virtuous, rather than vicious, cycles and to look for points of intervention where downward spirals can be reversed.

Operationalising risk

Much of this knowledge is familiar to researchers and to some policy-makers. But it is striking how rarely systematic analysis of these risks can inform the way that services and support workers actually operate. Too often, knowledge about patterns of risk remains untapped because it cannot be converted into forms which are useful in practice. Operationalising knowledge about risk factors and their conjunction is one of the major challenges for all agencies – public, private and voluntary – working with young people.

A second obstacle to making better use of risk profiles is the concern that it could lead to stigma and mistaken identification. The existence of a particular risk factor does not lead straightforwardly to a particular outcome or necessarily call for a particular kind of intervention. The assumption has often been that the precise lines of causation must be clearly identified and established before intervention is justified. If these conditions are not established, intervention must wait until after the event, by which time it is often too late.

A third obstacle is the fact that responsibility for different government functions – housing, education, health, employment and so on – is entrenched in departments and organisations with clear organisational boundaries. As we have seen, it is the conjunction of risks which creates and reinforces the greatest danger. But the types of information used by different agencies often relate only to their specific organisational remit. For example, although a teacher may well know about family circumstances that increase the risk of non-attendance or school exclusion, the formal records will lie with police or social services, who can only become involved once some has gone chronically wrong.

But as we will see from the evidence of what works, effective responses do not rely on mechanistic or automatic responses to risk identification. Instead, the lesson is that identification of risk should lead to a more detailed assessment of need and then to the creation of a specific package of support, a pathway out of risk which reflects the fine grain of an individual's situation. These packages are unlikely to be effective if they do not enjoy the consent and active support of the young people involved and of their families or guardians.

This view of risk analysis and its contribution to effective service provision implies a general framework for risk reduction. Its aim should be to improve available knowledge of different factors, trigger systems of support and contribute to the provision of effective and appropriate policies. It should also minimise mistaken identification and labelling, avoid hostile or unwelcome intervention and activate interventions that have the active support of young people and their families. The core elements of the framework are:

- an appropriate evidence base
- a system for identification of at-risk areas, groups and individuals
- appropriate forms of contact with at-risk individuals and, if necessary, their guardians
- full diagnosis of need, negotiated and agreed by professionals, young people and their guardians
- design of a package to stimulate and support virtuous cycles
- delivery of the package
- monitoring and evaluation of effectiveness.

This process, when it works successfully, can create its own virtuous cycle, since effective support that is properly evaluated contributes to the evidence base used for risk identification, and successful engagement increases the legitimacy and reputation of service providers with both the individuals involved and others who know them.

Opportunities and resources

In order to create virtuous cycles, we must be able to employ the appropriate range of available *resources*. As we have seen, one of the major contributory factors to marginalisation in early adulthood is the inability of the frameworks in which people live to make sense of the disparate resources needed for successful transitions to adulthood. This is true of the framework of educational institutions, the labour market and, for many people, the family.

But the public and policy debate about young people often overlooks resources which can be highly valuable. Where government policy is concerned, 'resource' far too often just means more money. The political, media and lobbying focus on increased public spending tends to obscure the fact that what matters is not just how much money there is but *how it is spent*. Alongside money and formal infrastructure there is a wide range of resources which young people need to consume and create in making successful transitions.

One way to think about this wider set of resources is to examine the research evidence on factors that help to protect young people against risks and inhibit rather than reinforce disadvantage. A range of long-term studies and programme of evaluations have identified a common set of characteristics that contribute to resilience in adversity. Although for many young people these resources are already present in an individual's life, for others, they need to be invested.[49] Some of the most common protective factors include:

- *strong relationships* with parents, family members, teachers or other significant adults
- *clear, high expectations and role models* provided by parents, teachers and community leaders
- *active involvement* in family, school and community life
- *feeling valued* – parents and teachers who value the skills and contributions of young people
- *individual characteristics* – outgoing and intelligent children are more likely to exploit opportunities and be resilient to dangers
- *persistence* and the ability to pick yourself up after failure.

These factors show that it is not just material resources and opportunities that make a difference. The relationships, cultural norms and social resources which families and communities can offer are just as influential. Figure 20 sets out the full range of resources which might be employed to support the development and transitions of a young person.

These resources are all present to some extent in most young people's lives.

Figure 20. Resources for development

Social	**Social networks:** depth and breadth of relationships with friends, family and institutions. Source of information, skills, comfort, and affection **Social cohesion:** sense of belonging and participation in wider community activities **Trust:** in people, places and institutions
Material and physical	**Housing quality** **Money:** to fulfil basic and higher consumption needs **Places, spaces and facilities** which can be used by young people
Knowledge	**Basic skills:** eg literacy, numeracy, computing **Life skills:** interpersonal, financial literacy, independent living skills **Work-related skills:** teamworking, communication, leadership, personal organisation **Credentials:** academic and vocational **Work experience:** depth, breadth and relevance to personal goals **Informal knowledge:** opportunities, sources of income and support, knowledge of different contexts, cultures, ways of being **Information and guidance:** knowledge of choices, options, consequences
Psychological	**Self awareness:** of strengths, weaknesses, desires, needs, **Self-esteem** **Self-concern** **Sense of future:** ability to set goals **Decision-making:** understand risks, consequences of actions **Entrepreneurialism:** exploiting resources, opportunities **Sense of independence and autonomy** = resilience, positive sense of self
Professional	**State services for youth:** teachers, social workers, family support, education welfare officers, educational psychologists, youth offending teams, drug action teams, counsellors, youth workers, careers officers, employment service personal advisers, GPs and health professionals
Cultural	**Norms, values and traditions:** which can help orient and ground a young person **Understanding of different contexts, perspectives, ways of doing things:** can help young people to communicate, modify behaviour, fit into different contexts **Cultural magnets and influences:** which can be harnessed to support and encourage achievement

For many, some are crucially absent and increase the risks they face. However, the crucial question is whether or not they are combined in ways that support and reinforce positive progression. Beyond addressing the most extreme forms of deprivation, the greatest gains will be made by moving towards a system in which the different forms of resource are woven together rather than working in isolation or at cross-purposes.

One of the reasons we are so easily trapped into narrowing the list of resources is that, for many of those listed above, it is impossible to offer them in the same way to everyone. The traditional assumption is often that public services should offer a consistent level of service and that this means standardised units of support, whether education and training places, benefit entitlements or public housing. For some forms of entitlement, this is undoubtedly true. But creating effective solutions depends as much on tailoring resources to fit the identity and needs of the individual.

A second reason is that some of the resources are intangible; it is much harder to measure the quality of a supportive relationship, the level and consistency of expectation, or the appropriateness of encouragement for a young person. These come from different and diverse sources. They do not fit our assessment frameworks and output measures.

A third reason is that many people take informal and intangible resources for granted. The job of the state, in this view, is to provide the tangible goods to which people are entitled, with suitable conditions attached. It is not possible to create or control these wider resources: they arise spontaneously from families, traditions and communities, and government and professionals should not interfere.

But none of this diminishes their importance. While government cannot directly provide or create the full range, it can work to create enabling frameworks which encourage their development. This means creating platforms and hubs around which other resources can be integrated, creating and disseminating knowledge about how it is best done, and rewarding effective forms of practice.

Understanding the full range of resources is a necessary step to creating effective support systems. It is the positive equivalent to understanding risks. However, the thing that really makes the difference for at-risk young people is the various ways in which these resources can be *combined and connected*, and the ways in which they *interact* with the needs, identities and activities of young people

Understanding the framework of support in these terms requires a new way of mapping the factors which make a difference. In general terms, we should be concerned with the relationship between young people's *needs and identities,* the *resources and provision* which can support them, and the *outcomes* we want their interaction to produce. This interaction can be mapped as a triangle (Fig.21).[50]

At any stage in an individual's development, there should be an appropriate balance between the three points of the triangle. In the case of off-register young people there are three main failures: the gap between identities and provision – or between what people need and what they get – lack of knowledge about outcomes. and the absence of a clear set of *outcome goals*: the objectives which represent milestones towards a positive transition. In order to improve coherence of the framework, three conditions must be met:

- establishing an agreed and balanced set of outcome goals
- identifying needs and potential, and creating systems that communicate them more effectively

Figure 21. A framework for support

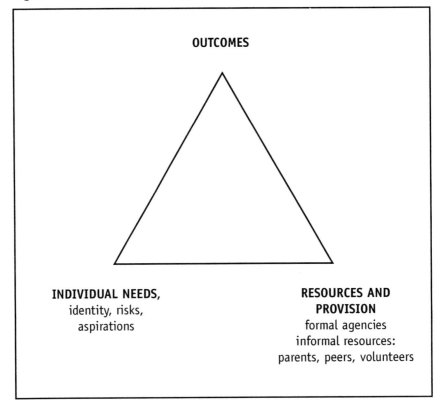

OUTCOMES

INDIVIDUAL NEEDS,
identity, risks,
aspirations

RESOURCES AND
PROVISION
formal agencies
informal resources:
parents, peers, volunteers

- combining the wide range of formal and informal resources available in ways which produce positive outcomes.

Only with a clear overall framework will it be possible to design effective supports and interventions for at-risk young people. But the arguments and evidence presented in this chapter are still relatively abstract. With these in mind, chapter four addresses a more concrete question: what works in practice?

What works?

Understanding the limitations of the system and the kinds of resources that people need is academic if the understanding cannot be translated into practice. This chapter sets out the things that seem to make a difference, and the ways in which some projects and programmes have approached the problems that young people face. The starting point is practical use of knowledge.

Creating and managing knowledge that works
Targeting and engagement
The first stage of reintegration is to establish contact: reconnecting young people to projects and people who can provide support. Many young people lack the knowledge, trust or inclination to seek out programmes at the times when they might be helpful. Some of the best projects have a proactive approach to finding and engaging with them.

Most young people at risk do not go unnoticed. Those who truant, commit crime or experience problems at home have often had contact with a range of agencies such as social services, the education welfare service and the police. Schools, too, often have concrete evidence of who is at risk through attendance and attainment records and contact with peers, siblings, parents and teachers.

The projects cited below vary in the type of knowledge used to target young people. Some use formal knowledge housed in agency databases, while others rely on informal knowledge of peers, professionals and volunteers contained in local communities and schools. One of the common aspects of the projects cited below is their success in *forging voluntaristic non-stigmatising relationships*. Targeting need not be associated with negative labelling and coercion – these projects do it by providing activities and support that young people value and trust.

Targeting: integrated information systems
Many of the most excluded young adults will have been known to agencies during childhood and adolescence, yet these interactions are recorded in the

separate databases of different agencies. A person who truants, has been arrested and has spent time in care will be on three different databases owned by the educational welfare service, youth justice and social services respectively. The fragmentation of records means that individuals with multiple risks often go unidentified. Agencies often work with the same individuals in isolation and sometimes at cross-purposes. Worse still, a person may be known to several agencies but receiving little or no active support. Somebody known to the police and education welfare service may have simply received a caution from the former and a couple of visits from the latter, despite being out of school for long periods.

An innovative approach to identification and engagement has been pioneered by Hertfordshire's Young Citizen's Programme (YCP). It consists of a tripartite database which pools information from social services, the police and the education welfare service. The database contains simple details about why the young person is known to an agency, for example school exclusion or truancy. Once identified as at risk, further information is obtained from the relevant agencies. The project also has a geographical mapping system which can identify clusters of at risk young people. The mapping system has highlighted several hotspots which could potentially be targeted through area-based interventions.

The programme targets young people who are known to two or more agencies. Before they contact the young person through his or her parents, YCP must get permission from one of the agencies that the individual is known to. Only after the parents give their consent is the individual contacted by telephone, letter or home visit. Commitment to engage with the project is purely voluntary, yet three-quarters of all young people targeted have agreed to take part. One preventive aspect of the project is the targeting of younger siblings for group work. In summer 1998, 100 per cent of siblings contacted took up the offer of support. The targeting of individuals or families is often thought of as stigmatising and intrusive but YCP has found that, once contacted, young people and their parents are often willing to participate. As one of team members said, 'When I knocked on doors as a social worker, parents were reluctant to cooperate – they had images of social workers taking their children away. Introducing yourself as from YCP, you are much more welcome.'

Although many organisations target young people known to agencies, they depend on referrals from frontline agency workers rather than access to single or integrated databases. Organisations such as Fairbridge, therefore, invest considerable effort in informing and gaining the trust of such workers through regular open days. For smaller organisations in particular this process is extremely resource intensive and, even then, many organisations complain that the referral process is deeply flawed. Professionals are often unaware of or mistrust other organisations' ability to work with some of the most difficult young people. Conversely, they can also use them as a dumping ground. Such referral systems also depend on active contact with workers from statutory agencies. Individuals who may be known to several agencies but are not in active contact are not in a position to be referred. Integrated databases, therefore, offer the potential for far more complete coverage of young people at risk.

Another approach to integrating information, developed by Leeds City Council, is to create a single claim form for the range of benefits – from free school meals to Housing Benefit and school clothing grants – and to connect this information to records of pupil achievement. This allows analysis of educational progress in relation to the socioeconomic circumstances of the family. It can therefore rank different schools in terms of which pupils are from disadvantaged backgrounds. The evidence generated has provided firm evidence of the links between those schools with large numbers receiving benefits and low GCSE performance. The information has been used in a variety of ways, including:

- analysis of 'value added' in schools
- analysis of the extent to which children of lone parents are receiving necessary support
- tracing the extent to which FE colleges and Leeds University are widening participation
- refocusing the work of the youth service in accordance with patterns of risk and need
- securing additional funding and planning regeneration initiatives
- community planning and needs analysis, and analysis of crime levels.

Integrating this information also opens up opportunities such as the pooling or front-loading of funds. The research shows that in one small part of the city, £12 million a year or £226,000 per week is paid in benefits to 1,932 households – a figure that does not take into account police, youth work, social service or school budgets.

The potential for integrating the vast stores of data collected by the range of administrative systems is immense. A range of other data such as careers service records, health data, training provider records and tax and national insurance records could all supplement information from schools, educational welfare, social services, youth justice and benefits records. From these, it ought to be possible to create comprehensive risk profiles of individuals and areas and to track progress from childhood into early adulthood.

But there remain considerable obstacles to integrating formal data. The first problem in developing the Hertfordshire system was data compatibility. Different agencies record characteristics such as gender and ethnicity differently and cover different geographical areas. The quality of information is also a problem: often YCP finds that it is incorrect or out of date.

As well as improving data collection, organisations need to be more open about sharing it. Individual agencies and services habitually hoard data. Many of the projects we talked to complained that some in particular, including grant-maintained schools and the employment service, are often slow to pass on information. For example, the St Mellons Community Centre in Cardiff fought a long battle to get the local employment service to release data on job vacancies. The main objection was that the employment service needed to know how many jobs they had matched in order to monitor their own performance. If targeting based on integrated information systems is to be developed further, improvements are needed in data quality and compatibility along with frameworks, protocols and formats for information sharing. The integration of personal information also raises major questions of data protection and privacy. However, there is now a relatively clear framework governed by the Data Protection Commissioner, which sets out the rules and conditions for use of personal data. When done with clear purposes and limits, and a right of subject access to data held by a given agency, there is no reason why more sophisticated databases cannot be created to support risk identification, targeting and service integration.[51]

Targeting: informal local knowledge
A complementary approach to formal databases is to tap into the rich local knowledge of peers, volunteers and community members. The Pennygraig Community Project in Wales, St Hilda's Partnership in Middlesbrough and the Matson Neighbourhood Project in Gloucester all mobilise these informal resources to target young people.

One project that has been particularly successful in this approach is Youthworks in East Lancashire. The project began in 1994 on the Roman Road Estate in Blackburn and has since spread to two other sites in the county. It places responsibility on volunteers who live on the estate. Although outside agencies such as police and social services also supply names to Youthworks, most of the targeting is based on the ground level knowledge of volunteers and peers. Local people who live on the estate have a far more comprehensive and nuanced picture of young people's activities and needs than youth workers or outside professionals. Volunteers are constantly in touch with young people. Listening and talking to young people provides invaluable information on what young people are doing and who may be risk. The volunteers we spoke to believed that there was hardly a single young person on the estate that they did not know.

The value of young people does not stop at identification of risk. When it comes to actually getting young people to come on a residential or take part in an activity, the perception of peers is vital. As the coordinator of Youthworks, Adrian Leather, says, 'Young people simply need to know whether an activity is good or not, and what time is it on.' This kind of 'hot knowledge', communicated through reputation and informal knowledge, is far more persuasive than formal information and contact. The use of peer targeting has included supplying young people with names to target and giving them parental consent forms to hand out. The distribution of hot knowledge need not be a purely random process – it can be a systematic and precise tool.

Seasonal targeting

A third of all crime on the Roman Road estate was being committed in the summer holiday period. Youthworks therefore targets this period by putting in place more intensive diversionary activities, including three to four day residentials and outdoor sculptures and murals. Crime on the estate has now fallen annually by a third for three successive years.

Another project that targets the summer holiday period is Tower Hamlets Summer University, set up in 1995 to involve young people aged fourteen to 21 with the double aim of boosting educational attainment and reducing crime. The effect on juvenile crime has been dramatic, reducing criminal damage by over a third and grievous bodily harm by half. The scheme has won widespread approval from many quarters. As one local beat officer said, 'Every summer for the past four years there have been fights and gang warfare on the estates here. But not this year; now we have the Summer University on the doorstep.' A parent commented: 'This is the first time my son's been out of bed before 1 pm in the summertime since he was in the juniors. This year he has been out of the flat by 10 am every day to go to the Summer University.'

Targeting and universality: seamless school services

Targeting young people is often associated with stigma because being singled out can label a person a failure. Avoiding the need for completely separate provision should be a priority. One project with an innovative approach to this dilemma is Youthlink in Surrey, which has demonstrated how customised specialist support can be provided within a universal framework.

Set up in 1986, Youthlink is managed by Surrey Education Services and works in a number of schools. The key components schools are an inter-disciplinary team consisting of an educational psychologist, youth worker, teacher and education welfare officer, based in a room in the centre of the school which is open to all young people. The main aim is 'to work with targeted young people identified as difficult, disruptive or disaffected within a school environment.' Targeted support is embedded in universal services connected to young people's personal and social education. This includes a range of extra-curricular activities such as day trips, sporting activities and residentials or simply using Youthlink as a common room and a place to talk to adults who are not teachers.

Around fifteen young people in each school also receive more specialised support such as family mediation and counselling, and occasionally a full alternative curriculum. Targeted individuals have a specific action plan but in practice a wider range of young people benefit from the guidance, support and brokerage provided by the Youthlink team. When we spoke to the young people who used the Youthlink room and participated in activities, they did not know which of them were receiving more targeted support.

Youthlink targets young people on the basis of many sources of information. Heads of year pass on information from the teaching staff, social services, youth service and educational welfare service, and information is sometimes received from peers and parents. Young people are also targeted through regular contact between Youthlink staff during extra-curricular activities. Many teachers and parents are aware that certain individuals are at risk of failure or non-attendance but there is usually no channel for communicating this knowledge and taking preventive action. Young people, too, need channels through which they can communicate their own special needs or those of others. By having a targeted service so closely integrated with universal school provision, Youthlink manages to act as a hub for a wide range of information and support.

Tracking

Young people's transitions from post-compulsory education are often marked by mobility. They can ricochet between insecure or informal employment, training schemes with low completion rates and the benefits system. As we have seen, they need more continuous support and quicker responses to changes in status. This cannot happen without more continuous monitoring. Tracking is also essential for evaluating continuous improvement strategies.

The need for tracking has been recognised by the government. A wide range of data systems monitor young people's status at local and national levels.

- schools' census and LEA information on attendance, exam entries and achievements
- further education colleges' individualised student records, held by the further education funding council
- TEC management information databases on young people in government-supported training
- Higher Education Statistics Agency student records
- careers company information on pupil destinations after leaving school
- National Insurance and Benefits Agency records
- social services client records
- youth justice records
- education welfare service records
- health records.

The data required to keep in touch with young people and target those at risk is largely in place. Although there is some data sharing, for example between LEAs and Careers Service companies, the overwhelming picture is of fragmentation. One attempt at creating a more comprehensive system is the Coventry and Warwickshire Tracking Project, set up in 1994 by the local TEC. The project expanded the existing careers service database by merging it with other information from the TEC, LEA, schools and FE colleges. In order to pool the data, a common unique identity number for each individual was agreed upon and given to everyone in year 11 and software developed for exchanging data. The project achieved early identification of young people dropping out of the system and a more accurate picture of the links between qualifications and post-sixteen destinations. However, the project also points to a range of problems. First, young people moving into or out of the area evade the tracking system. Second, young people moving into employment or unemployment are more difficult to follow up because the project does not access benefits or National Insurance records.

The Coventry project tries to track the whole year 11 cohort. An alternative approach is to focus on particular groups of young people identified as at risk. This is the approach taken by the South Glamorgan Action on Missing Youth Programme. One component of the programme, On Track, works with 60 young people in two schools during year 10 and 11 identified as at risk of dropping out of school or getting low grades. Once they have left school they will be tracked for two years with regular meetings with careers advisers, sometimes as often as once a week. More generally, South Glamorgan is targeting young people who enter status zero and tracking their progress thereafter. An individual identified as out of work, training and education is then tracked over the next two years. Again, young people who enter employment are likely to lose touch with the system. Alongside the integration of public data systems, the relationship between employers and public agencies supporting young people is crucial to providing sustained support. Creating the right connections with employers is a question that we return to later in the chapter.

Evaluation and dissemination

Although there are many signs that some projects are making an impact, rigorous evaluation, especially of long-term outcomes, is still relatively rare. Many practitioners, particularly in small-scale, community-based projects, justifiably complain that they do not have the resources to invest in evaluation. This is partly due to funding pressures and a focus on short-term outputs. But it also reveals a general belief that evaluation is at best a chore and at worse a threat. Auditing is largely viewed as a process carried out by outsiders for the sake of outsiders rather than an opportunity to learn and improve.

However, there are signs of change. In line with trends in the private sector, it is becoming more widely recognised that auditing is should be done by insiders as well as outsiders and continually rather than occasionally. The growth of a performance culture across the public and voluntary sectors is beginning to have an impact on provision for young people.

The focus on tracking young people and data integration creates new opportunities to measure the 'distance travelled' by individuals and areas following particular interventions. YCP's geographical mapping system can trace whether hotspots of truancy, exclusion, family conflict and youth offending have been affected by the project's work. The project team can also trace the progress of young people they have worked with up to the age of eighteen through its database.

Agency and administrative databases are useful for evaluating concrete and long-term changes. But these records do not show more subtle, intimate changes such as changes in self-esteem, interest in education or work, family relationships, friendships and patterns of drug use.

For these more complex pictures, a wider range of perspectives is needed. The most direct and authoritative source of information and evaluation is young people themselves. Various measures can be used to factor young people's views and judgements into the process of evaluation. Wakefield Council has established a practice of exit interviews for all care leavers. Other projects involve young people in neighbourhood forums and service user panels. As one study of the characteristics of effective neighbourhood youth projects in US cities showed, opportunities for leadership and involvement in decision-making are a key characteristic of effective projects, contributing to individual development as well as to the responsiveness and positive ethos of projects overall.[52] Similarly, youth consultation contributes to more sophisticated evaluation of different forms of provision.[53]

In Tyneside, the Key Fund provides small grants to groups of young people with proposals for community-based projects and initiatives. Hundreds of schools, voluntary organisations and youth projects across the UK are developing similar forms of practice. Involving young people as active creators of solutions, both for themselves and for others, is a vital part of the process.

Personal action plans are increasingly used to help structure and tailor support to individuals, and also create frameworks for measuring progress and generating evaluation data. The process of planning an individual's programme, reviewing its success and feeding the lessons learned into the next phase development is key to achieving progression. The Big Issue in the North, a programme for homeless people based on individuals becoming vendors of *The Big Issue* magazine, has developed an innovative system for monitoring the progress of vendors who sign up to their Big Step programme. Individuals are assigned a caseworker and formulate action plans which chart progress on five main fronts: substance use, housing status, education, employment and psychological well-being, according to a scale of one to five. As well as structuring and mapping progress for individuals, the format generates knowledge about the relationship between the five different factors.

This model, which integrates user assessment, organisational records and evidence for wider outcome evaluation, points out the direction for evaluation and assessment regimes. Along with forms of evaluation that are embedded in the direct work and data systems of organisations, there is also a case for better external evaluation. In this respect in particular, there is a lot to learn from other countries, especially the United States. These evaluations are usually conducted by organisations that specialise in evaluating programmes and disseminating the lessons, such as public–private ventures and the Manpower Demonstration Research Corporation, of which there are no direct equivalents in the UK. Strengthening the relationship between research evidence, practice and policy formulation in youth provision is vital to improving the effectiveness of the overall framework. The recently launched Research, Policy and Practice Forum on Young People is a welcome start.[54]

Implications

Engaging and supporting marginalised young people depends on the creation of knowledge bases around new units of integration. While evidence and statistics exist at national aggregate level, and often within the records of specific agencies, it cannot be used effectively unless it is generated, stored and used in forms which can be used *in practice*. Much of the knowledge about what works is currently held informally by practitioners and young people themselves. As with other resources, it is the ways in which knowledge is combined which makes it useful. This depends on bringing together disparate strands of information, and synthesising and communicating them in different ways.

The sources range from agency and administrative data, informal local knowledge, professional and research-based evidence, and the perspectives of young people themselves. Combining them helps to achieve several objectives simultaneously.

The focus on knowledge management has important lessons for the development of professional practice. It shows that effective strategies rely on the *pooling* of knowledge from different disciplines and that, despite the localised and informal settings in which these workers operate, systematic collection and review of data are essential. Creating an underlying evidence base, and stronger forms of information exchange about good practice, are the platforms on which professional discretion and knowledge can be based.

Working with young people

Winning the commitment of some of the most disadvantaged young people is not easy. Sustaining it is even harder. Projects often have to overcome a deep sense of mistrust and alienation. But without a strong commitment to a project, progress is unlikely. Young people will not simply be fed through a programme – they need to good reasons to attend: the people, activities, services and other incentives that they offer.

But engagement is only the first step – the best projects make substantial differences to young people's lives. The need to engage young people and ensure that they progress can be in tension. Sometimes projects create a sense of dependency or artificial expectations that will lead to stasis or regression. But ultimately progression and engagement are complementary. Without a sense of progress, young people often lose faith in the purpose of a service or activity. From the projects visited and studied there are a range of characteristics, tools and models which make a difference.

Voluntarism

It is often argued that programmes which rely on voluntary participation will not reach the most excluded because of their disappearance or disaffection. But voluntary, mutual relationships are a vital part of projects and programmes which support longer-term progression.

Take Youth at Risk as an example. This organisation works with some of the most marginalised young people – in a 1998 programme in Knowsley involving 29 young people, over two-thirds had been excluded from school, all had been arrested at some point and over half took drugs on a daily basis. Yet this group of young people volunteered for a week-long intensive residential and a nine-month follow-through mentoring.

Youth at Risk uses volunteer enrolment teams to recruit young people through outreach work. Volunteers, rather than professionals, often have the time and the ability to engage young people. As one young person said, 'You know with volunteers that they're not just talking to you cos it's their job – they're talking to you cos they care.' As another put it, 'Social workers try to put words into your mouth – these lot ask questions.'

The second key feature is persistence. Youth at Risk will often try to convince a young person on several occasions to join the programme. Commitment is always voluntary, but the offer is made several times. This kind of approach has caused concern: the programme as a whole radiates an air of missionary zeal. For the staff and volunteers it is integral to the determination to make a difference. As one volunteer said, 'You have to be more persuasive than simply sending out a letter or two – you need to have face-to-face contact and you need to give them several opportunities to come on the programme – you wouldn't get private companies just giving up on customers like some agencies do with some young people.'

Youth at Risk is just one organisation that manages to engage young people voluntarily. Hertfordshire's Young Citizens' Project is another with remarkably high success rates – over three-quarters of the young people targeted decide to participate in the programme. The Dalston Youth Project, another successful mentoring project based in East London, also works only with those young people who choose to participate and is consistently over-subscribed.

To achieve sustained involvement, voluntary engagement and trust are not enough – some tangible attraction or benefit is an important part. Projects need to be either enjoyable, relevant or rewarding, and preferably all three. Whether they use targeting, referral or rely on reputation and word of mouth to draw people in, all successful projects rely on some form of *magnetism.*

Cultural magnets: sport, art, music

Some of the most engaging projects harness the power of culture to attract and retain young people. Cultural activities are usually designed not just to divert young people but also to enhance skills, self-esteem and status. In other words, the magnet is used as a medium for broader personal development. Many are also characterised by opportunities for leadership and responsibility that they confer on young people – to organise activities, work in teams, develop new skills, and maintain disciplines such as time-keeping, attendance and effort.

Immtech is a music-based pre-vocational training provider based on an industrial estate in Cardiff. The attraction for young people is the opportunity to make music in high-quality studio facilities. It has developed a key skills course moulded around making computer-based music and aims to act as a feeder for more mainstream training providers. The projects has clear disciplines – young people have to turn up on time otherwise they cannot stay on the course and there is a financial reward for completion. This helps to create regular working routines. It aims to boost self-esteem and the ability to work in teams, and helps divert young people away from destructive behaviour. The course has one of the highest success rates in South Glamorgan for getting people on to mainstream vocational courses. Of the 91 young people who worked with Immtech from April to September 1998, 80 went into full-time education, training or employment. Immtech has developed close links with particular employment-based training providers who receive over 70 per cent of trainees into employment.

Immtech is just one of a number of projects that uses music to reach young people. Making Music Work, run by Northern Recording in Durham, targets young people between the ages of fourteen and 21, with a particular emphasis on the young unemployed. It provides free access to a range of facilities and project-based teaching in all aspects of the music industry. It is currently establishing a virtual record label to distribute the work of regional bands through the Internet and is working closely with six secondary schools and the youth service to get more young people and teaching staff involved.

Another cultural magnet is sport. Organisations such as Reach for Success, the Youth Charter for Sport and Fairbridge show how sporting and outward-bound activities can often engage young people that colleges and training courses fail to reach. Reach for Success, in Teesside, targets young people in primary and secondary schools and in housing estates through basketball. Sporting and other cultural activities can provide enormous motivation for young people, at the same time as encouraging disciplines and skills which can be transferred to other spheres. They can help raise self-esteem, forge relationships with peers and adults, and teach particular skills, be they specific, such as computing, music or multimedia, or more general, such as interpersonal and teamworking skills. At the same time they divert young people from anti-social activities. Not all young people have an automatic interest in organised sport, music, arts or multimedia. The same principles of engagement, voluntarism and careful progression apply to effective projects, but these examples illustrate the power of cultural resources to infuse structured programmes with a motivating quality that is often missing from more general institutional frameworks.

Financial magnets

Many projects use some form of incentive to attract, retain and reward young people. Some are more implicit than others. Projects such as Youth at Risk, Fairbridge and Weston Spirit offer intensive activity-based residentials as the starting point for longer-term work, particularly mentoring. The initial attraction is clear enough: as one girl who went on a Youth at Risk residential put it, 'I thought it were a holiday.'

Other programmes use more explicit incentives. The Quantum Opportunities Program in America worked with 100 young people in five areas of America between 1989 and 1993. The programme involves a range of activities including computer-assisted education, community service and mentoring by adults over a period of four years. They make strong use of financial incentives. For each hour of activity, a young person receives $1.00, rising to $1.33 over time, for up to 750 hours in a year. After completing 100 hours, participants receive a $100 bonus and an equal amount is invested in an account that can be used for QOP-approved activities such as college or training. The programme has achieved significant outcomes: over 60 per cent completed the four-year programme, and compared to the control group 26 per cent more people went on to post-secondary education, with one site achieving a 48 per cent improvement. Other outcomes include a 14 per cent drop in teen parenthood, improved skills levels and a more hopeful view of the future. As the co-founder of the programme, Ben Lattimore, says, 'How do you treat your kids? You reward them when they behave well and punish them when they don't. It's a simple idea, really, but it works.' The YouthBuild programme, based on a similar model of credit accumulation alongside new forms of participation, relationship and achievement, has also been shown to have a significant positive impact.[55]

Other programmes have a system of graduated rewards. The Big Issue in the North gradually introduces vendors to higher rewards coupled with greater responsibility over time. For example, the reward for commitment and progress in an individual's development plan might be gaining fast track access to housing association accommodation. If things go wrong, the vendor will have to bear the risk and responsibility. The structure of incentives can usefully underpin a programme by creating a series of clear challenging targets and tangible rewards for hitting them. They complement, rather than replace, high-quality work with young people but they can play a crucial role in raising expectations, commitment and self-esteem.

Magnets: work and income

One of the central shifts in the nature of the transition from child to adult is delayed economic activity. Work not only provides income and independence – it is a source of structure, status, skills and socialisation. Many young people would like to access these job opportunities much earlier, yet the labour market is often restricted. Social economy projects such as the Arts Factory in Wales, the Matson Neighbourhood Project and the Big Issue, show that labour market opportunities can be created even for the most vulnerable young people. These organisations provide work directly, while others, such as the Chance to Work in Liverpool, help to broker opportunities with existing employers.

The Big Issue is a particularly interesting example because of the nature of its client group. Over 60 per cent of *Big Issue* vendors in the North inject drugs on a daily basis – many vendors would struggle to sustain a job in the formal economy or make the transition into independent tenancies. Yet the Big Issue illustrates that some form of economic activity can be compatible with risky and vulnerable lifestyles. Work, if it is timed and structured in the right ways, can help to stimulate the positive changes in health, self-esteem and motivation, which strengthen efforts to reduce drug dependence. As one vendor on the Big Step resettlement programme said, 'When I started selling the magazine, I found it hard work, but the money helped me to pay for drugs – before I was a vendor I had to steal … since the GP has been here, I've got completely off the heroin and I'm taking less and less methadone. I reckon I can get right off it.'

The Big Issue offers a very different model to the conventional linear transition from education to employment that still dominates most approaches to marginalised young people. It suggests that some form of economic activity can accompany and stimulate rather than follow broader changes in individuals' lifestyles and capacities – that conventional divisions between earning, learning and personal development should be broken down. Projects that offer meaningful economic activity for marginalised young people are still few in number, but sheltered opportunities in the labour market may offer numerous advantages for the most vulnerable in terms of income, status, structure, self-esteem and skills.

Magnets: quality services

Projects such as Big Step, The Hub in Bristol, Bypass in Bolton and the Arts Factory in Wales show that high-quality, relevant, accessible services can be a good way of making initial contact with young people and a preliminary to more structured support. The Big Issue in Manchester has a GP surgery, an IT suite and housing advisers located in its basement. The GP started work in August and within six weeks there were over 150 homeless people registered, half of whom were *Big Issue* vendors. This service did not need to be marketed heavily – knowledge spread through word of mouth. The GP acts as a magnet because of the demand for methadone prescriptions. The service now means that many homeless people can access health care before problems reach crisis point and before they end up in casualty departments. The GP service also acts as a lead-in to the other services, which are situated next to the GP surgery.

Other lead-in services include a drop-in advice centre that is situated where the vendors collect magazines. Staff say that informal unstructured contact with staff members and attendance at drop-in sessions is often a precursor to more structured personal development plans. The caseworkers also say that the vendors who do best on the more structured programme tend to be those who have signed up to Big Step after having accessed the drop-in on a repeated basis.

The Arts Factory in Rhondda, Wales, has a diverse range of activities ranging from free legal advice, which have proved particularly popular among young men, self-defence classes and mother and toddler groups for women and large-scale music events. These activities have not only provided advice, guidance and recreational activities for young people – they are also a way of reaching those who may not know of, or be initially attracted to, Arts Factory's training and employment opportunities. These kinds of services, particularly recreational and entertainment services, require credibility. Arts Factory brokers deals to allow local bands to play in pubs – the offer of staff, reassurance and insurance can open up opportunities and diversionary activities that young people would find hard to negotiate independently.

The Hub in Bristol was established in 1995 in response to reports highlighting Bristol's homelessness problem. It is a one-stop shop containing a range of state and voluntary services including the employment service, social services, careers service, housing services, Avon Health Authority, the Benefits Agency and voluntary organisations such as Shelter, Bristol Cyrenians and the Bristol Drug Project. The project draws large number of phone calls and visits – it sees over 230 new people a month and 650 overall. The ground floor is run by the voluntary organisations which act as the gatekeepers, referring homeless people on to relevant teams upstairs. They aim to create a more welcoming atmosphere and have expertise working with particular groups such as asylum seekers and people who have been illegally evicted.

The one-stop shop provides all the services an individual may need in one building and allows different agencies to come together easily – case conferences can be called within the hour. The bundling together of different services also means that different services within the building cannot dump clients on to each other, although outside agencies still tend to use The Hub as a dumping ground. The Hub model shows the multiple benefits which front office integration can achieve: improved flexibility, profile, ease of access and interdisciplinary working.

Positive relationships

Building or mending relationships is a complex and fragile task. Many of the most marginalised young people face huge barriers in managing relationships because of negative experience and limited past opportunities for personal and social development. But interactions with parents, teachers, friends and mentors are a crucial mediator of positive behaviour and success. Many projects therefore focus on creating and strengthening these bonds.

Intensive residentials and mentoring

An increasing number of schemes, including Youth at Risk, the Dalston Youth project and the Weston Spirit, make use of one-to-one relationships between volunteers and individual mentors. These relationships are often forged and strengthened through intensive residentials.

Youth at Risk's week-long residential is an extremely demanding experience, both physically and emotionally. At the beginning of the week the participants write down the things they want to change in their life – three of which are posted on the wall. Most days involve a variety of physical activities like ropes courses and trust exercises which have a visible impact on the young people's morale and sense of achievement. Throughout the physical exercises participants have to re-affirm their three key aims, for instance, just before jumping off the top of a ropes course. The physical sessions constantly get young people to exceed their expectations. They are designed to require patient, sustained effort. The coaches, volunteers and other participants push the young people to constantly overcome fears and inhibitions. The atmosphere is always one of high celebration of any achievement.

The evening sessions involve what is controversially known as 'confrontational therapy'. These sessions go through several stages through the week – at first the sessions try to get participants to confront their behaviours, background and identity in front of others. This tends to be a highly moving, difficult but cathartic experience. The sessions then try to build the participants up – teach them to appreciate themselves, to care about the future and create a sense of personal agency – a belief that their actions have clear consequences and that these actions should be in line with what they really want out of life. The emphasis throughout is on individuals taking responsibility and control over what they do.

The residential also introduces the participants to their mentors through games and exercises over several days. As one mentor said, 'It's no use just introducing a mentor to a young person for an hour or two – you need to have some intense sustained experience to build some kind of bond.' Mentoring schemes often forget basic facts about how relationships are formed – intensive residentials are ideal opportunities to build new relationships with adults. A further important feature of quality mentoring is the training of the committed partners – they receive a similar experience to the young people on the residential in order to understand what the young people will go through. Although the residential begins the process of changing individuals' behaviour, the hard work is done over the following nine months, during which the group meet weekly in the evening and for a whole Saturday each month.

Youth at Risk's approach is, in some respects, similar to the Dalston Youth Project, although the nature of the residential is somewhat different. These intensive behaviour-changing courses seem to have a valuable impact on some of the most high-risk young people – most of whom have already had contacts with the criminal justice system. At present, access to such high intensity courses is minimal in most localities.

Mentoring helps to fill a gap in many young people's lives: trusted adult support and guidance. The growth of mentoring schemes in the UK has been swift over the past ten years. Systematic evaluation has shown that mentoring can make a significant preventive impact but attention must be paid to training, matching, and sustained support for both mentors and mentees[56] The creation of a mentoring infrastructure requires time and effort but is a crucial part of a wider framework of support.

Family mediation

Poor family interactions often lead to leaving home at an early and vulnerable age and, in some situations, to homelessness. Problems are diverse – they range from the abuse, neglect, parental ill-health and substance abuse to conflict born out of competing demands, difficulty with step-parents and sibling rivalry. Many projects come across situations which, though severe, can be substantially improved. Providing family mediation services through skilled and trusted others can help to prevent the escalation of difficult situations to crisis point.

Several projects, such as Youthreach in Derbyshire, Youthlink in Surrey and Hertfordshire's Young Citizens' Project, undertake flexible problem-solving family work. It largely involves investigating what is going wrong, trying to reach some kind of compromise between different family members and providing sustained but low-key follow-up support either with the family as a whole or with particular members. It might also mean assisting family members to achieve personal goals that may indirectly improve family interactions. This may involve linking them up to a local college or, in more severe cases, to mental health services. The striking feature of projects such as Youthreach is that the work is determined by the individual problems rather than set routines or defined functions. This approach might mean giving telephone support at any time, or taking a mother who has very low self-esteem and lack of social contact to a local women's centre. As one social worker said, 'They can be so much more flexible than we can. They can go shopping, find accommodation, look through the paper with them for jobs, help filling in application forms. Whatever is necessary.' A crucial part of the role is helping to mediate between family members and helping to reach clear, sometimes written, agreements. As one young person put it, 'To be honest, it was the first time I had ever had a say in any meeting. They asked me what I wanted. I could make things how I wanted them.'

Brokers

The crucial role that shines through from the diverse activities of almost all the projects we have studied is that of *brokerage*. Whereas most public agencies are geared around single functions and statutory responsibilities, brokers take on the task of connecting individual needs with wider supports and resources and their role is sustained over time, even when the situation changes as a young person passes through different stages of activity and development. Brokers such as Youthlink and YCP combine a variety of skills in multi-disciplinary teams that allow them to meet shifting needs over time rather than passing an individual on to a new profession.

Brokers' work is characterised by proactivity, prevention and early intervention rather than crisis work. The ethos of both YCP and Youthlink is to try and remove as many obstacles and blockages as possible, being flexible about the timing of meetings and going out and visiting families rather than referring them to a family support centre. The lesson is that trusted, flexible intermediaries play a vital role in negotiating the fault lines between different services, institutions and opportunities.

Perhaps most crucially, projects such as Youthlink manage to connect young people up to opportunities that they would otherwise miss out on. Facilities and schemes such as study support centres and the Duke of Edinburgh Award Scheme are used by large numbers of young people but often the most marginalised do not take part. These wider opportunities are still funnelled through the school and its staff, so if this relationship is poor, young people are unlikely to take up wider opportunities. By focusing on developing relationships that go beyond the usual teacher-pupil boundaries, Youthlink has managed to get disproportionate numbers of young people with school problems to access wider learning opportunities. As one young person said, 'I wouldn't have been in school but for Youthlink – they were wanting to exclude me and nobody would give me chance … I now make use of the study support centre – I wouldn't be able do my GCSE work without it.'

Employment brokers

The brokerage principle also applies to employment. Employment linkage programmes act as a bridge between employers and jobseekers, providing many of the sustained support functions that fall between state and employer provision. Such projects recruit, screen, prepare and support disadvantaged young people for placements in the private sector. They provide a pool of labour for employers, helping to save on the costs of hiring and initiation, while providing young people with access to jobs and support that they would not find alone.

In the United States, employment linkage programmes have been shown to help those with the least access to work, such as the homeless and those with no work histories. For instance, in 1995–96, the Neighbourhood Employment Network in Minneapolis, Minnesota, placed 1,706 people in jobs, of which approximately three-fifths were considered high or very high-risk candidates because of their work histories and personal challenges. Another example is the Milwaukee Careers Cooperative, which in 1995–96 placed 1,132 people in jobs out of 2,053 who went through intake interview and orientation. Employment brokers have the potential to help improve young people's access to jobs and ensure that spells of inactivity are relatively short. Temporary work can be a useful way of gaining experience and skills, particularly if they can help to provide continuity between young people's fragmented experiences of the labour market.

The Hunter Valley Labour Co-op is an Australian example of a similar idea: a not-for-profit employment agency established in Newcastle to help young people gain access to casual work under more secure wages and conditions.[57] Individuals are employees of the Co-op, which then lease workers to employers. The fact that it was established by the trade union movement points to the role that the British labour movement could potentially play in helping to create solutions for these young people. Similar intermediary functions are provided by a range of American programmes, including high school career academies and others designed to support welfare-to-work schemes.[58]

These organisations can also help to provide labour market information in more efficient ways. As well as building up detailed knowledge of their members' interests and skills and therefore adding value to the placement process, intermediaries could help to integrate and disseminate information about vacancies, particularly through on-line networks. Organisations like YouthNet in the UK are pioneering a new approach to integrating information for young people. Creating job information networks that pool vacancy data from job centres and employers, labour market forecasts, odd-job and casual work opportunities along with reference information about education, training and entitlements would be a major step in linking young people with opportunity.

There is no reason why education institutions themselves should not be involved in developing these intermediary structures, as they develop their place in a wider infrastructure. Young people increasingly combine work with study and growing numbers succeed in developing entrepreneurial ideas and establishing businesses. Why should schools and colleges not act as bases and brokers for these forms of economic activity? Creating these hubs of job-focused activity would also provide a base for the informal networks of hot knowledge which influence young people's ideas and decisions about work and opportunity. The experience of US careers academies, which help to integrate peer group membership, school-based learning, sustained work experience and mentoring, provides another set of lessons for the development of practice in the UK.

Because of their nature, the scale and value of the informal and illegal economies are hard to quantify exactly. There is little doubt, however, that informal activity plays a large part in the lives of many marginalised young people. All of the participants in the Real Deal consultation had experience of informal work and a smaller number had at times made considerable amounts of money working in the drugs economy. This involvement, while damaging both to communities and to the life chances of individuals, is nonetheless the training ground for skills and knowledge which could, potentially, be put to constructive use in the legal labour market. A recent survey found that working children contribute 2 per cent of total family income and 6 per cent in families on Income Support.[59] While children from affluent families are more likely to work, those from poorer families work longer hours for lower rates of pay. Understanding young people's involvement in work before they leave the education system, and the ways in which it can be tied to positive pathways rather than becoming a barrier, should be an urgent priority.

In Britain, neighbourhood organisations such as the Matson Neighbourhood Project in Gloucester and St Hilda's in Middlesbrough have shown how local intermediaries can provide information, advice and training, and sometimes more intimate support such as transport or maintaining a link with an employer. Matson's employment linkage service managed to get over 100 residents into jobs by the end of 1996. Consequently, unemployment fell in that year by 38 per cent, half of which was directly the result of Matson's service.

The key element in linkage services is the development of networks with employers and potential employees and the ability to provide advice, training and support for those who enter a job. Organisations with a strong local identity and staff are in a much better position to foster contacts with local people, but developing links with employers can often be a challenging task. In order for such organisations to develop the necessary networks it is important that bodies such as the employment service, chambers of commerce and TECs provide the necessary support and information. If organisations are to maintain their links with employers, they must be seen to be providing a valuable service, such as extra support, training and screening of employees.

Flexible pathways

Brokering achieves little if structures are inflexible. Brokering usually requires some form of compromise or deal – a new working arrangement that both sides are happy to uphold.

One such example is the last two or three years of education. For a significant minority, this period becomes characterised by truancy, exclusion or failure. Around 7 per cent of young people leave school with no GCSEs, while figures for truancy and exclusion appear to be rising. However, some projects have demonstrated that this group of young people need not end up out of education and with little future. A range of projects such as the South Glamorgan TEC's Youth Access Initiative, Step Forward in Derbyshire and Youthlink in

Surrey are creating alternative curricula for some of the most disaffected young people – usually those who are out of school for long periods. These curricula often involve flexible arrangements whereby an individual may spend some of the time in school or college and other periods in work-based training environments.

The Alternative Curriculum Project, part of South Glamorgan TEC's Youth Access Initiative, has a highly flexible programme whereby an individual will spend anything from one to five days with a training provider and the rest of the week in school. Programmes are formulated on the basis of mutually agreed plans following an interview with a training provider. Each programme is tailor-made to the individuals with regard to literacy, numeracy, IT and work experience based on a combination of information from the school and the young person. A total of 108 people took part in the programme last year with overall attendance of over 90 per cent, despite the fact that all the young people had not been attending school prior to the programme, in one case for over two years. The 222 qualifications gained by the group ranged from word and number power through to NVQ level 1. The 97 students who have now left the programme have had very positive outcomes: 78 per cent have gone into training or employment, and the rest left the programme early. This alternative curriculum is now being applied more widely in South Glamorgan. Creating new pathways, particularly from fourteen on, can clearly have a dramatic effect in engaging young people in education and training who have previously been non-attenders.

There is an obvious danger that alternative curricula can become an excuse for shunting difficult young people out of schools. Whether they do depends on the quality of the guarantee which young people are offered, and the level of connection between the hub of activity and a range of other providers. If alternative curricula are to be genuine learning experiences, they must involve tailored programmes that bring together different learning experiences in different settings – with training providers, specialist support services, employers, schools and colleges.

The alternative curriculum is a good example of providing a new rung on the ladder that can attract and retain young people with negative experiences of school-based education. Another example highlighted earlier is Immtech, a pre-vocational music-based provider that is also part of South Glamorgan's Youth Access Initiative. This project engages young people who are not in work, education or training through the attraction of making computer-based music. The jump between status zero and mainstream training provision is one that needs bridging. The key with projects such as Immtech is to provide an attractive and accessible enough course to attract the most marginalised young people but also provide some kind of leg-up to the next rung on the ladder – so that young people progress to more mainstream courses. Immtech has proved to be particularly successful at both attracting and moving on young people to positive outcomes. Projects such as this suggest the need for more courses that bridge the gaps in provisions and smooth the process of reintegration.

Overall lessons
The lessons from our study of pioneering organisations, new forms of practice and evidence from abroad show that a difference can be made to the problem of off-register youth. The key themes to draw out are as follows.

- A high-quality information infrastructure is essential to improving the effectiveness of provision. Although vast amounts of relevant information are stored in a range of institutional repositories, they are not properly used because they are not combined in formats that are accessible and relevant to the clusters of risk which indicate danger of marginalisation.
- Informal networks of knowledge across agencies, neighbourhoods and communities are an essential complement to the underpinning infrastructure of institutional knowledge. Strategies for combining these different forms of knowledge are urgently required.
- The skills involved in working with marginalised young people are complex and sophisticated, requiring flexibility, the capacity to build trust and the ability to operate in informal and semi-formal environments. These skills are possessed by a wide range of professionals and volunteers but they are not systematically recognised or rewarded.
- Proactive targeting of individual young people is an essential part of engaging those at risk. Such targeting nonetheless depends on the capacity to form voluntaristic, non-stigmatising relationships based on negotiation, persistent effort, and mutual respect.
- Points of engagement are primarily local and depend on openness and accessibility, the integration of a range of functions and services, and the capacity to create longer-term progression from a series of intermittent, casual and low-trust initial encounters. Crucial to this process is the ability to establish some kind of positive relationship with each individual.
- Pathways towards positive transitions need to begin well before the point of transition itself. Sustained, flexible combinations of activity, particularly ones that wrap around basic provision such as school, offer the best

chances of preventing complete detachment from work, learning and mainstream institutions.

- Short-term attractions and rewards, such as relevant cultural activity and financial incentives, are a key part of building longer-term progression.
- The range of skills and capacities which surrounds formal educational attainment – personal and interpersonal skills, emotional development, time management and learning to take responsibility – are often foundations which have to be laid before, or alongside, more formal provision.
- The role of brokerage between families, institutions, opportunities and different resources is fundamental. This role is insufficiently recognised and supported in the provision core public services, particularly education and job search.
- The right combinations of support and activity can produce 'double dividends', reducing crime and drug use, creating positive social outcomes, raising skill levels, preventing unemployment and preventing the need for more expensive interventions after crises have occurred. The cost of these packages should be compared against the cost of the full range of negative outcomes that they help to reduce, rather than simply against standard forms of education and training.

We now turn to the question of how a national policy framework could reflect these lessons and, in the long term, make a sustained impact on the off-register problem.

A framework for inclusion

This report has shown the extent of a largely hidden problem: the numbers of young people who, in passing from childhood and compulsory education to adulthood, lose their place in the social, institutional and economic framework that provides opportunity and stability in adulthood. The extent of their presence has been difficult to prove because of the way that the state categorises and counts people. The evidence in chapter two is the first national estimate of the numbers of young people not in full-time work, education or training and not claiming unemployment benefits. The data is imperfect and probably underestimates the scale of the problem. Some of the young people who show up in these statistics are choosing not to participate and we still do not know enough about their reasons and motivations. But it is clear from the evidence we have that their marginal status represents a grave danger, for two reasons. The first is that it has a negative long-term impact on their life chances. The second is that, given the increased likelihood of economic inactivity, crime, poor health and homelessness, the wider costs to the taxpayer, employers, families and local communities are also huge.

A new policy consensus has begun to emerge in the UK, focusing on the importance of early prevention for combating social exclusion and marginalisation. This is surely right. Policies to reduce child poverty, improve early health and education support, raise literacy and numeracy levels and reduce crime are essential. But they will not achieve their goals unless the framework of services and support for young people also changes. In any case, early preventive policies will not touch those young people who are already marginalised. While some have talked of a 'lost generation', there is no need to give up on the idea that these young people also have the capacity to participate, to achieve independence and to contribute to society. Longitudinal studies have shown that not all of the variation in people's life chances is determined by background and early childhood factors.

Our research, and that of others, has shown that there are effective responses to marginalisation. The question is whether we can adjust our expectations and our policies to respond effectively.

In this final chapter we set out a new framework for inclusion. The argument is that over time it could go a long way towards reducing the scale and cost of the problems we have identified. It would help to engage those currently on the margins, and also to prevent the flow of young people into off-register status in the future. Its overriding aim would be to create structures and supports which work *together* to enable positive long-term transitions for those most at risk. Its effectiveness depends on the whole system of support, from national programmes and government departments, local agencies and partnerships, community and neighbourhood organisations, families and individual young people working in concert. Our analysis has identified six key objectives for such a system:

- from an early age, *target support and resources* towards those most at risk
- *engage young people* through better combinations of magnets and resources
- *track young people over time* to provide continuous support and rapid response to changing status
- provide a range of *customised routes* for progression which meet all young people's needs, now and in the future. These should enable each young person to build up the range of capital: material, knowledge, social, cultural and psychological, which they will need to thrive
- provide young people with brokering support: to mediate between family, opportunities and services and knit together fragmented resources
- evaluate the long term effectiveness of work with young people
- fund and reward services according to their effectiveness.

Beyond single interventions
Too many efforts at reform in this area of policy begin with the supply side: seeking to make the existing system more productive without changing its parameters. This tendency contributes to the problems of fragmentation, incoherence and incomprehensibility that young people's services already suffer from. A new system must be rebuilt around the needs and identities of young people growing up now.

Within the current infrastructure, many efforts are under way to improve the quality of individual services: schools, careers services, youth offending teams, social services, employment advice, college courses and so on. Among these, the most promising reforms are those which create a framework which can *combine* different forms of support. At the largest scale, this is the aim of the

New Deal. At the local level, projects like the ones we have examined bring together opportunities and resources in new ways.

Understanding stages of development

In order to achieve independent adulthood, young people need a series of clear stages through which they can pass. These stages are partly determined by institutions: primary and secondary school, college or training, employment and university. But these tend to work best for those who are already doing well. The classic middle-class transition from school to A levels to university provides structures which allow not just steady accumulation of qualifications but also opportunities for socialisation and personal development in a partially sheltered and supportive environment.

For young people who cannot gain access to these frameworks, the routes to contribution and fulfilment are far less clear. The support, guidance and advice systems that should be there to help are often only available to those who know how to make use of them and who trust the professionals and institutions which run them. A recent study of the factors affecting decisions at sixteen found that six out of ten young people would have liked more help in making decisions about post-sixteen options. Half said that they would have liked careers lessons earlier. Lack of advice and guidance was one of the most consistent criticisms emerging from the Real Deal consultation. It is all too easy to see how the vicious cycle of marginalisation and disaffection can take root.

Better traditional institutions are not enough. This is because people increasingly *combine* activities rather than follow a linear sequence. Work, formal study, parenting, training and time out can all form part of an individual's programme of development. As lifelong learning becomes more important to employability, people will need patterns of provision which allow them to integrate learning and support into increasingly diverse lifestyles. The range of service providers will continue to diversify. Distance learning through information technology means that individuals are no longer tied to a specific geographical area or single institution. The youth labour market no longer provides long-term security or regular routines: economic activity is more fragmented and disjointed. The challenge is not to push young people through particular programmes, institutions or discrete stages, but to *weave together* activities and opportunities across the key transition points. This process helps to smooth transitions, reducing the number of abrupt changes which take place simultaneously. As opportunities become more individualised, we must ensure that they are available to more than those who have been given a flying start in life.

What young people need
Creating pathways
In order to marshal the resources and steps required for positive transition, we need a framework that is simple enough to be coherent and universal, and flexible enough to be adapted to individual needs and circumstances. The concept which brings these together is the pathway: a structured, coherent route to independence.

> In choosing a pathway, members of a community agree about the goals of the system and the steps to be taken to achieve those goals. Such planning involves a determination of what should occur at every age and grade level, and how that set of practices fits into the broader picture.[60]

The pathway is much more than the choice of a pre-defined route. It involves careful construction and coordination of a wide range of different resources. It extends beyond the bounds of a singe institution like the school into social, economic and community life. A clear pathway, supported by guidance, staging posts and markers of achievement, is the underpinning structure that every young person needs in order to negotiate their way through the risks and opportunities of the teenage years. It creates a shared responsibility between individuals and provides them with support.

Into the idea of a pathway can be integrated the opportunities and guarantees that society should offer to each young person. These might include:

- high-quality education or training
- adequate material security
- effective, sustained guidance and support
- the availability of a mentor
- a range of positive role models
- opportunities for employment, volunteering and responsibility.

There would be a range of pathways on offer, some beginning at fourteen and all continuing for at least five years. All would include qualifications but they would be achieved through different combinations of activity and experience. The main pathways might include:

- a full-time academic pathway, combined with limited work experience and extra-curricular learning opportunities
- an apprenticeship-based pathway, run through partnership between

employers and education providers

- a carer's pathway, combining childcare, part-time study and work
- a young entrepreneur's pathway, providing capital loans, business mentoring, volunteering opportunities and learning credits
- an arts, design and culture pathway, combining accredited learning, apprenticeship in the relevant industry, and opportunities to display and perform
- a civic pathway, combining learning and community involvement.

Each of these pathways would include intensive placements or courses within their structure, for example during vacation periods or between course modules.

Personal frameworks for recording progress and achievement

For individuals to combine these different forms of activity into a coherent whole, they need a common framework for recording and rewarding objectives, achievements, progress and entitlements. This is not just a question of developing monitoring systems, but of new ways to develop, assess and accredit the broad range of skills and personal capacities which all young people need. This could be achieved in the following ways.

Individual learner registration numbers

A unique identity, assigned near birth to every child, which forms the backbone of all administrative records throughout an educational career. These records should be anonymised for all uses in which individual identification is not essential and should be made fully and freely available to learners and their families at frequent intervals. Relevant information should be collected on needs and risk assessments, membership of institutions and service programmes, accredited qualifications and key milestones.

Individual portfolios of achievement

A universal portfolio developed and legally owned by individuals, which records details of progress and achievement in education, training and employment. This would build on the National Record of Achievement currently used in secondary education. It could be IT-based and each institution or provider enrolling a learner in a course or programme would carry a responsibility for maintaining it and making it available. The portfolio would be the main portal for the transfer of relevant information at transition points throughout a learning career. It might eventually be linked to Individual Learning Accounts and the Personal Job Account, creating a framework for all major transactions between government and citizen.

Skills and curriculum

New forms of skills assessment are needed which reflect the range of generic skills, and personal capacities which contribute to employability, independence and the ability to thrive. As Pearce and Hillman argue, a unified qualifications framework for fourteen to nineteen year olds should be a medium-term goal.[61] However, greater attention to a wider set of characteristics and capacities, particularly personal and interpersonal development, is needed.

The Real Deal consultation project identified life skills, relationships and a broader curriculum as a key aspect of education felt to be missing from young people's experience of school. A range of good practices has emerged in this field and is reflected in the recent review of personal, social and health education and the introduction of a new statutory entitlement to education for citizenship and democracy.

Creating new training and resource bases for provision in these areas should be a priority for schools, local authorities and the Department for Education and Employment.

The pressure on schools to meet targets in more standardised forms of attainment and to deliver all aspects of the National Curriculum should also be acknowledged: coverage of subjects remains the enemy of depth of understanding and the need for broader personal and interpersonal development must be recognised in future reforms of the curriculum framework.

More sophisticated and reliable ways of integrating key skills development and assessment into the whole curriculum should be found. The National Record of Achievement and some portfolio-based awards such as ASDAN and the Youth Achievement Award represent the most promising routes to this, accompanied by wider involvement in assessment and accreditation, for example, by employers.

A recent study of the views of employers in Tyneside found that vocational qualifications came thirteenth on the list of desirable attributes among young job applicants, behind qualities such as ability and willingness to learn, reliability, trustworthiness, initiative, literacy and verbal communication. As one employer put it:

The gap between how they present themselves on paper and how they present themselves when they're here is so big that I'm wondering whether a lot of schools and careers advisers spend a lot of time on the paper person and not much time on the interview person.[62]

Time accounts

Time is one of the most precious resources and most basic dimensions of any young person's development. Yet time management and accounting are systematically neglected in the provision of services, support and learning. This is largely because mainstream institutions for young people have their routines pre-programmed through timetables.

From secondary school age onwards, each individual would receive a time account which they would use to plan and record their time use and accumulate credits. Particular activities would accrue credits that could be spent on a range of activities including education and training courses, discounts for leisure facilities and consumer goods, childcare, residential courses and so on. Time accounts would become a key tool in linking together different forms of activity, including spells of temporary or casual work, and helping to ensure sustained progression and reward for achievement. Time planning and personal organisation would become a key part of the hidden curriculum in all educational provision and pathways.

For example, a young person with a particular interest in cars might be able to gain credit for the detailed and specialist knowledge that he acquires – this could be connected to out-of-school activities, perhaps involving working in a garage or re-assembling stolen motorbikes as at the Youthworks project. A person working in a shop on a Saturday morning might be able to do a project in school researching customer demand for the products they are selling and learning more about a particular sector. A young carer may be able to earn credit for her caring duties – possibly through linking it to some kind of qualification in childcare that could involve evening classes or distance learning to fit the learning around her time constraints. Volunteering, for example through the government's Millennium Volunteers scheme, would also be included.

Time accounts would require greater partnership between schools, employers, voluntary organisations and recreational services. To work, an individual would need an account manager who could broker different time arrangements and help to align different activities. They would be linked to the portfolio of individual achievement and potentially recorded through smartcard schemes, which would put learning credits, leisure entitlements and other forms of information literally in a young person's pocket, following a similar structure to supermarket reward schemes. Some entitlements would meet national standards, for example in earning future education credits. Others, such as access to leisure facilities and consumer discounts, would depend on local partnerships.

Providing material resources

Alongside these individual frameworks and tools, government should introduce a single common entitlement to fund programmes and packages designed to support completion of education to eighteen, vocational education or the entry to full-time work with training attached. The level of the funding entitlement should be equivalent to the cost of two years of post-sixteen education, since this is what most off-register young people are missing. However, it should be spent more flexibly, enabling specific packages of support to be designed and delivered.

A single education maintenance allowance, currently being piloted by the UK government, is a desirable long-term goal, payable to all young people participating in full-time training or education whose family income is below a certain level.

Childcare entitlement should be automatic for any sixteen to 24 year old carer re-entering full-time education or training. The subsidy for working parents planned under the new Working Families Tax Credit will not be enough to provide support for many off-register mothers who are living alone or with workless partners.

Government should support the development of integrated support packages for homeless young people and care leavers. These should focus on:

- developing effective pre- and post-transition strategies and brokering support from the range of statutory agencies
- supporting agencies which provide effective brokerage and guidance services alongside direct provision such as housing or education
- accrediting local and specialist agencies to act as intermediaries in negotiating and holding housing and unemployment benefits on young people's behalf. This accreditation would depend on a high level of trustworthiness and transparency in auditing and publication of outcomes for the agencies concerned.

Targeting and tracking young people at risk
Knowledge management systems

Coordination of services and provision of individualised pathways can only work effectively at local level. Further development of systems that integrate and cross-compare different sources of data, such as those developed in Leeds and Hertfordshire, should be strongly encouraged. A Canadian example is the Multi-Agency Preventive Programme for High Risk Youth in Manitoba, a crime reduction partnership based on the sharing of information between the youth justice system, family and children's services, and schools. Management and coordination of local knowledge should become a strategic responsibility of local government, in partnership with specific agencies and service providers. This responsibility would include:

- developing social and economic profiles of local areas and neighbourhoods to support need and risk identification, allocation of resources and youth strategies
- managing the integration of data sets to help target and stay in touch with those individuals and households most at risk, using data from schools, social services, police, probation services and so on
- releasing anonymised integrated data sets for more detailed studies of patterns and dynamics of risk
- collecting and learning from outcome data as part of a continuous improvement strategy for the provision of services
- helping to allocate resources to and to sustain strategic partnerships with the range of service providers contributing to individual packages of support.

These systems will take years to develop to the point of a comprehensive national system. All, however, can be piloted and refined at local level.

Coherent public service strategies

Creating coherent patterns of public service provision depends on the existence of clear youth strategies at a local level. While national government structures play a part, the level of coordination which matters most is *the local*. Many local authorities already have well-developed strategies for young people but many more do not.[63] The plethora of statutory plans and strategies, including children's services, education development and community safety strategies, seem in some areas to be contributing to the lack of coherence in services for adolescents. Introducing a new statutory duty for youth development strategies would probably not help. However, local authorities should be encouraged to develop more coherent frameworks, particularly in family and social services, for supporting vulnerable young people. The danger is that combined pressure and overload will continue to push local authorities into acute and crisis management work, with a negative effect on preventive work for young people.

Central government can support the creation of more coherent strategies by providing better strategic advice and guidance, encouraging dissemination of evidence from innovation, and providing seed funding for partnership initiatives. The Learning Partnerships announced in 1998 to support the development of lifelong learning strategies are a step towards more strategic coordination in local areas. Like all centrally initiated partnerships, however, they run the risk of being dominated by the main institutional providers and failing to draw in a wider range of partners. The seed funding for partnership provided by the government's New Start initiative is a more promising model for encouraging genuine strategies to emerge.

Other central government mechanisms which can encourage coherent strategies include:

- Block funding of consortium approaches and partnerships. The 1994 US National School to Work Opportunities Act provided for federal grants to states offering integrated programmes of support for the transition from high school to work and has encouraged greater strategic coordination between providers.
- Creating financial incentives for joint problem reduction based on genuine outcome measurement and gradually moving away from output-based measures of funding for specific services. One possible incentive is to re-allocate a small percentage of cost savings in negative budgets such as crime and unemployment benefit as a reward for problem reduction. These monies could be placed in local *community investment funds*, whose allocation is decided by local forums including young people.
- The benefits of pooling budgets to encourage flexibility in developing youth strategies should also be considered. Employment Zone pilots are the most promising source of innovation and lessons in this area.
- There should be a renewed emphasis on eliminating marginal differences between the regulatory and reporting regimes for different providers. Many of the differences in audit process, information management and reporting requirements between schools, colleges and other education providers stem simply from the fact that they have different histories. Although some of these formats are imposed from above, local providers can also work horizontally to establish common norms and eliminate differences which are of little value.

Overall, the role of central government in the long term should move further towards the creation of a coherent overall regime. Central coordination of Departmental initiatives, through a Youth Policy Cabinet within Whitehall is one possible route towards this. This would be led by a **Minister for Youth** whose primary responsibility would be the promotion of coherence across the range of policy, in conjunction with promoting and disseminating evidence on the effectiveness of strategies and approaches in different areas (see 'youth brokers' below).

The need for better partnership is also a major challenge for **voluntary and community sector** providers. Better knowledge management should contribute to clearer coordination but it is partly a question of ground-level providers grasping the nettle. As Frances Ianni puts it:

> *The lack of coordination among youth programmes has roots in the basic inclination to protect one's own turf. Every agency has a speciality, a catchment area, a* raison d'être. *Every profession has its own area of expertise. Every brand of school reform has its own philosophy, its own principles and methods. Every youth programme has its own twist. And the people who run the agencies, reform efforts, and programmes have jobs and egos to protect. Many of them believe that they have the answer to troubled youth. They are suspicious of, if not downright unfriendly to, others who may approach the problem from a different angle.[64]*

A recent audit of three housing estates in north-east England found over 30 different professionals from more than ten different agencies all claiming to be working with disadvantaged young people. Most did not know about the activities of most of the others. Effective strategy depends on the readiness of youth professionals and organisations to lift their heads and engage in wider debates and strategies with each other.

Mobilising community resources

Alongside these formal structures, wider community engagement is a priority. Involving a wide range of adults and community institutions in clarifying expectations of young people and helping to create solutions is a vital part of the effort to re-engage. One tool for doing this is the 'youth charter':

> *The youth charter is an approach that brings together all adults who are in positions to influence young people – parents, teachers, town officials, police, clergy, sports coaches, club leaders, counsellors, new media, employers – in the quest to define high community standards for youth development. A youth charter focuses on the core features of character and competence that young people need to acquire in order to become responsible citizens.[65]*

The process of debate, discussion and mobilisation that leads to a youth charter is as important as the terms of the charter itself. It is a focal point for clarifying people's concerns, opening up discussion and establishing shared goals. It is part of the process of making the whole environment coherent and consistent for young people, and of involving the wider community in supporting and evaluating young people's progress. Often these processes are initiated by social entrepreneurs working informally but they require wider participation and institutional involvement to make a real impact. Several local areas in the UK have introduced youth charters. Perhaps the most notable example is the Youth Charter for Sport in Manchester. Youth and young people are issues which motivate and concern most people. When an approach is found which allows them to participate constructively in finding solutions, the response can often be surprising.

Auditing local resources

Broad-based consultation and dialogue can help mobilise resources that could otherwise lie unused, such as volunteers' time, physical spaces and facilities. This process is also supported by systematic public and community auditing. For example, the Pennygraig Bridges project has converted two unused houses, donated by the local housing association, into a flexible space that is used by children and young people, and managed by volunteers from the local estate, particularly young mothers.

At a different level, better understanding of public spending flows is also needed. A recent pilot study found that spending on sixteen to 24 year olds is markedly less in deprived areas than in more affluent ones, largely as a result of higher education spending, which tends to go to middle-class families.[66] The same study found that money going into deprived areas is more likely to be 'ameliorative', for example benefit payments, than 'investment'. Mainstream programme funding is, in the end, most influential in determining the quality of opportunities available to young people. Understanding the dynamics of this spending at local level, rather than simply up and down national budget lines, should be a priority. Both these types of audit are easier to pursue when information and knowledge are managed in the ways described above.

Developing local infrastructure

Given the importance of location and scale for the success with which local projects engage marginalised young people, there should be a sustained drive towards developing an infrastructure of neighbourhood youth projects, local economic brokers, one-stop shops and lifelong learning centres. This layer of accessible, connected infrastructure is a fundamental part of a new system.

Out-of-school learning

The infrastructure for out-of-school learning should be further developed, building on the National Framework for Study Support. This includes opening access to libraries, community learning and study support centres, museums and IT centres. Creating a learning infrastructure that is more accessible, open for longer and connected to a wider system of opportunity and entitlement is vital to finding ways for many outside the mainstream to re-engage. A 1995 report by the US Department of Health and Human Services found that students who spent no time in extra-curricular activities were 49 per cent more likely to have used drugs and 37 per cent more likely to become teen parents than those who spend one to four hours a week in out-of-school hours learning.

Full service schools

Schools remain the community or neighbourhood institution with the most universal and influential presence for most young people. Whether or not they will be the sole provider of learning and support services, they have an important part to play in retaining contact and helping to make information and opportunity accessible to young people. The growth of 'full service schools' in the United States has shown the considerable potential for integrating services and opportunities around the school as community hub. For example, in New York a partnership between the Children's Aid Society and the City School Board has stimulated the creation of several schools where education is co-located alongside health, recreational, family, pre-school and social work services.

The scope for community engagement, preventive service provision and involvement of families and parents in learning, voluntary and employment projects is greatly enhanced. For young people living in workless households, these service networks and forms of wider community attachment are particularly important. Career Academies within schools which help to integrate formal learning, work-experience and mentoring also form part of this institutional development.[67]

Economic activity

The relationship between positive progression for young people and economic activity can hardly be overstated. As well as basic job opportunities and income, unskilled young people have lost the structures, norms and forms of group membership that past forms of employment offered.

Creating more effective *intermediary structures* and *employment umbrellas* can help to connect demand with supply and help create ladders for young people towards security in the modern labour market. This means support for local projects that help to stimulate economic activity, for mutual and cooperative organisations that provide pre- and post-employment support and for information networks and stronger employer partnerships.

The typical labour market experience for low-skilled young people is not linear in the way that educational careers still are. The new form of employment security – employability – relies on the individual's ability to make sense of a fragmented set of opportunities and demands, without the stable organisational structure which conventional employment once offered.

The role of employers is crucial here. The workplace as a context for learning is far more likely to provide motivation, role models and rewards for young people with negative experiences of formal education. The OECD has argued that employer-led vocational education and training systems are associated with an average four per cent reduction in youth unemployment levels.[68] The establishment of National Training Organisations for different sectors, already under way in the UK, is one step towards this goal. Further development depends on creating single area-based institutions with responsibility for employability and skills development. While enrolling employers in national programmes such as the New Deal is valuable, the identity of employers as local community institutions is probably even more important and should also be drawn on. In particular, creating local systems that involve small- and medium-sized enterprises as well as large employers is vital.

Such steps depend on flexible local networks of cooperation and intermediaries rather than on subsidies, tax incentives or large-scale formal agreements. The functions they could help to stimulate include using employees as volunteers and mentors – the next stage for responsible employee involvement in the new youth labour market. Such links will reflect local conditions and rely on networking and entrepreneurialism.

Part of the challenge is to find ways of providing continued progression from early starting points through different stages of work. Many off-register young people have pre-vocational needs. Their need for support will go beyond entry into a job, since jobs do not guarantee progression on their own. This is why qualification *and* guidance structures which span the transitional stage between education and secure employment are so vital. Finally, government must recognise that, in the end, inclusion depends partly on the existence of work opportunities. Developing strategies for employment generation which go beyond crude demand management or make-work schemes is another long-term challenge.

Working with young people

Alongside the emphasis on information management, we need a new focus on *effective* youth work. A clear theme emerging from the examples of projects and programmes that make a difference is that at least one adult has found a way to establish a positive relationship with the young person concerned. The skills of working with at-risk young people are complex, sophisticated and often misunderstood. People who do it well come from a wide range of backgrounds: youth workers, teachers, police, probation and careers officers, social workers and so on. But the skills and knowledge base of effective youth work have not been systematically assessed or recorded, and as a result practice remains highly varied. Youth work as a 'profession' remains veiled in mystery, despite the first national audit of youth service provision in 1998. Many youth workers do an excellent job in difficult circumstances. Others have been caught in their own form of marginalisation, left behind by neglect and cuts in services, isolated from other similar professions by mutual indifference and ignorance, and reluctant to examine their practice critically through a combination of ideology and fear.

Where teachers have traditionally had their professional practice defined by the need to impose a body of knowledge on young people as students, youth workers often see their job as dealing with what young people bring to them in less formalised settings. As a result, the imposition of structure or expectations on their encounters beyond a minimal level is sometimes resisted. This process of informal engagement is an important part of the job but it is not enough to contribute fully to young people's potential for longer-term transitions. The danger is that, operating at the frontline of young people's engagement with the wider system of provision and social expectation, youth workers can be captured by what they perceive as the young people's interests and perspectives. In many cases, this capture comes from motivations which should be respected, but in the end it limits the scope for progression and development.

This situation is not surprising, given the systematic neglect and downplaying of the status of the youth service in many parts of the UK over the past two decades. However, it will not be addressed simply by increasing their funding and profile. The failure of cooperation between statutory and voluntary youth services in many areas also presents serious grounds for concern. In short, the vital place of youth work skills to re-engage and support marginalised young people depends on real investigation of the state of practice in the youth work field and on placing the skills and knowledge base on a more secure and self-sustaining basis.

A youth brokerage service

We recommend that government should set an objective, within ten years, of creating a new profession: the *youth broker*, responsible for supporting young people in creating pathways to independence. Despite the bewildering range of professionals who may come into contact with vulnerable young people, there is currently no one responsible for the overall coherence of the support that they receive. Fully qualified in the skills of working with young people, the role of this profession would primarily be brokerage, helping to design, evaluate and secure combinations of activity and support that meet the full needs of any one young person. They would be based in schools, colleges, youth centres, voluntary projects and other locations used frequently by young people. Their roles and responsibilities would include:

- maintaining regular contact with young people
- collecting and analysing progress and outcome data: helping to sustain the knowledge and evidence base
- designing and actively brokering pathways
- reporting on the quality and coherence of pathways offered by different providers and partnerships
- assisting in training and monitoring the range of professionals and volunteers working with young people
- providing guidance, counselling and support
- acting as a source of information, referral and access to the range of services, opportunities and entitlements that a young person might need.

This national service would, for the first time, create a body charged with improving the coherence of services for young people across the board. It would be independent of any one profession or body of institutions, and should not be created out of any of the existing bodies inspection or regulatory agencies. It would help to separate the functions of advice and guidance and strengthen the status and knowledge base of professional brokers and guidance counsellors.

This form of support should be available at fourteen and earlier for those at great risk. It could be created through the long-term merger of the youth, careers and education welfare services.

In time, this structure and the people working within it would inevitably become influential, both in reporting on the quality of provision and in helping to set the future direction of youth policy. Its power should develop only in proportion to its effectiveness, and it should be under a legal obligation to publish and disseminate the evidence on which it based its decisions. As such it would be providing three basic functions:

- monitoring and supervising young people's rights and entitlements
- maintaining and improving the knowledge and information base
- managing and developing the provision of guidance and brokerage.

This overall structure, reporting on the quality and coherence of support for young people, coordinated at local, regional and national level, would be one of the pillars of the public service framework. It could also provide the organisational base on which the responsibilities of a Minister for Youth would rest. If provision of young people's services, especially training and education, continues to move towards diversification, competition and contestability, with a growing number of providers offering a wider range of options, then creating such a service is essential for ensuring that young people do not fall through the cracks. It would act as a spine for the whole system and underpin the guarantee that society should offer to every young person, including those most at risk.

This service should also play a key role in developing the scale and quality of *mentoring programmes*. Again this is a long-term challenge, but the repeated offer of a mentor to any at-risk young person who wants one is a key part of the framework. The growth of mentoring should be accompanied by the creation of an accreditation scheme for *youth ambassadors and champions*: individuals who make a sustained voluntary commitment to supporting young people in their transition to adulthood.

Young people as solutions
The final part of the picture is the recognition that young people can play an active part in creating solutions not just for themselves as individuals but also for other young people. They can be productively involved in many different ways in providing services, advice and mentoring, service evaluation, outcome measurement, teaching, and learning and innovation. Practice is piecemeal but it is growing steadily and forms an integral part of the new infrastructure.

At the Tower Hamlets Summer University, young people work as peer ambassadors, helping to recruit others and advise them on available options. The Centrepoint peer education project trains young people with experience of homelessness to facilitate learning in schools about the reality of homelessness and the sources of support and information which can be drawn on. At the Nucleus, in Derry, young people work as peer educators providing information and advice about drug and alcohol use. Some members of the Real Deal consultation are now developing an advice and facilitation service, providing guidance and training on how to run effective consultation with young people.

The knowledge and experience gained in living with the reality of disadvantage and marginalisation should be seen as resources rather than barriers, as long as effective support enables young people to overcome them. A part of this process is their conversion into the ability to support, and communicate with, other young people facing similar risks. These forms of involvement should be available to all young people and should be accredited and rewarded alongside other forms of learning and achievement. They contribute to self-management and interpersonal skills, as well as to a sense of involvement and motivation which are vital to positive progression. It is also worth recognising that, for those most distrustful and sceptical about the efforts of government to reach them, other young people are the most influential sources of information. For young people, projects and programmes which work are validated by reputation among peers, rather than by performance data or communication campaigns. A campaign of re-engagement, if it works, should ripple outwards to those who are hardest to reach, rather than trying to coerce them back into a system which has offered little in the past.

Alongside these benefits, effective consultation with young people improves the quality of service provision. Effective structures and systems for integrating the perspectives and views of young people into the decisions that affect them are therefore another long-term objective. The new National Curriculum entitlement to citizenship education creates an important opportunity to develop good practice in schools. Local youth forums and service-users' panels, regional youth parliaments and national structures for consultation on legislative proposals and national policy initiatives should also be developed. Government should also support the creation of a *Youth Consultation Development Unit* to develop and disseminate good practice and advise on how central government departments can involve young people in policy development.

In loco parentis

A crucial underlying theme of the report is the profound influence of family life on the prospects of young people, during adolescence as well as childhood. Always a dangerous and controversial area, governments have traditionally resisted direct intervention in families. Many of the social and psychological resources needed by at-risk young people are ones which stem from the quality and security of family life. This is partly why preventive and supportive frameworks are so important in the long term. But the lessons from what works also point to a new kind of approach for government: an enabling, supportive, brokering role, rather than just setting the rules and standing back or attempting directly to control and manage behaviour through the assertion of authority. This is particularly true for young people in a lifestage where they are testing out new experiences, roles and possibilities, where direct control is often counterproductive, but where lack of guidance and structure helps to halt progression and exacerbate risk. Government's role is partly to help create the conditions under which families can provide such support. But for young people who do not enjoy family support, the state also carries a broader responsibility, to act as an adviser and guardian, and to help marshal the resources needed for progression. This new relationship carries a risk of over-prescription and control. But its absence too often leads to serious isolation and exclusion. We should learn from the fact that attempts to provide such a role are only effective when they are characterised by relationships of trust and mutual respect, and where young people are actively involved in taking responsibility, creating their own solutions and evaluating outcomes. These are the checks and balances: qualities rather than formal rules or safeguards, which help to moderate and legitimate the role of the state. Fulfilling this role is not just a challenge for government, but also for communities. To a great extent, the problems of marginalised youth will remain unsolved until all community members play a more active part in supporting their development. This is less a question of taxpayers' money, and much more one of time, attention and recognition.

Conclusion

We have argued that tackling the problems of off-register young people is an essential part of achieving a cohesive society in the longer term. For much of the post-war period, work for low-skilled people allowed the prospect of at least incremental improvement in living standards, material security and independence. Changes in the social and economic framework mean that this is no longer the case. While most people will survive, mere economic subsistence is not enough to ensure any kind of progression or achievement. The changing rhythms of economic life, and the protracted period of transition that young people now pass through on the way to adulthood, create new risks of marginalisation, leaving people outside the mainstream with no clear route back in. As a young person in the Real Deal consultation put it:

> I think, I mean just getting in. I've managed to get into the system. I think
> there's a lot of help to be done in just getting into it. I mean I've spent a
> couple of years completely outside it all, didn't exist as far as anybody else

was concerned. And now I'm on the road to getting where I want to go. And once you get into the services and you find out and connect to one thing you can connect to everything, but if you never connect to the first part then you never ever reach any of that.

We have also argued that it is possible to create a system in which everybody gets the opportunity to thrive in adulthood, and the support and guidance necessary to make the transition. The four key elements of this system are:

- knowledge and information: who is at risk? what works?
- coherent pathways: providing combinations of activities which lead to progression
- brokerage: a new supportive role to help access opportunities and weave resources together
- wider community mobilisation

Creating the structures to support inclusion is a major challenge. In the long run it will arguably save money and certainly improve the quality of life in many communities. Reducing the numbers of young people not in education, employment or training should be a long term goal similar in status to increasing the numbers going to university: a marker of progress, and a reflection of society's overall priorities.

But there is a choice to be made. Most off-register young people will survive one way or another. Some will manage to put together a coherent progression of their own. Others will remain hidden, and the costs of their situation, though huge, will only be measured indirectly. Reaching and engaging them depends on our readiness to be *proactive:* recognising the problem, finding and engaging young people, rather than just responding to those who are willing to seek out help and support.

Many of these young people are disaffected and disillusioned. They are distrustful of professionals, politicians and public agencies. But their aspirations are no different from most other people's: they want homes, jobs and families. The overriding message of the Real Deal consultation was that, if some are disaffected, this results from the lack of support and interest they have experienced from the rest of society. As one person put it:

If they did a bit more research about what was going on in our heads they [would] know what else to do instead – if they cared a bit more.

A campaign for re-engagement is based, in the end, on our readiness to establish relationships with these young people. Without that form of positive human contact, no amount of extra money, training places or job opportunities will make a difference. This means an investment, not just of money and effort, but also of time and attention. Given the consequences of inaction, the case for making such an investment is difficult to resist.

Notes

1. Pullinger J and Summerfield C, 1998, *Social focus on the Unemployed*, The Stationary Office, London.
2. Payne J, 1998, *Routes at 16: Trends and Choices in the Nineties*, DfEE Research Report no 55, Policy Studies Institute, London.
3. DfEE, 1998, *Young People in Jobs Without Training*, Research Report 75, DfEE, London.
4. Labour Forces Survey, winter 1997.
5. DFEE Statistical Press Notice 471/98, The Stationary Office, London, 15 October 1998.
6. Examination achievements by gender in *Regional Trends 33*, The Stationary Office, London, 1998.
7. Information supplied by the Department for Education and Employment.
8. See note 7.
9. See note 5.
10. OECD, 1998, *Literacy Skills for the Knowledge Society*, Organisation for Economic Cooperation and Development, Paris.
11. Pullinger Summerfield, 1998, (note 1).
12. 'The consequences of drop-outs on the cost-effectiveness of 16-19 colleges' in *Oxford Review of Education*, vol 24, no 4.
13. Kiernan K, 1997, *The Legacy of Parental Divorce: Social, economic and demographic experiences of adulthood*, Case Paper 1, London School of Economics, London. Divorce used to mean all parental separations.
14. Graham J, 1998, 'Comment on John Bynner's paper' in *Comprehensive Spending Review: Cross-Departmental Review of Provision for Young Children – Supporting Papers*, volume 2, HM Treasury, London.
15. Welfare Reform Focus Files: Children and Families, Department of Social Security website
16. See note 15.
17. Hills J, 1998, *Income and Wealth: The latest evidence*, Joseph Rowntree Foundation, York.
18. *National Dwelling and Houshold Survey* and *Survey of English Housing*, 1995.
19. Jones G, 'Leaving the parental home: an analysis of early housing careers' in *Journal of Social Policy*, vol 16.
20. Jones G, 1995, *Leaving Home*, OUP, Buckingham.
21. Jones, 1995 (note 20).
22. *The Big Issue in the North: Annual Survey of Vendors 1997*, Manchester, 1998.
23. Strathdee P, 1992, *Sixteen and Seventeen: no way back – homeless sixteen and seventeen year olds in the 1990s*, Centrepoint Soho, London.
24. Taylor M, 1995, *Unleashing the Potential: Bringing residents to the centre of regeneration*, Joseph Rowntree Foundation, York.
25. Pullinger and Summerfield, 1998 (note 1).
26. Rural Development Commission, 1998, *Rural disadvantage – understanding the indicators*, Rural Development Commission.
27. Home Office, 1997, *Young Prisoners: A thematic review of HM chief inspector of Prisons for England and Wales*, Home office, London.
28. Rutter M and Smith DJ, eds, 1995, *Pyschosocial Disorders in Young People: Time trends and their causes*, J Wiley, Chichester.
29. Cooper PJ and Goodyer, 'A community study of depression in adolescent girls: estimates of symptom and syndrome prevalence'.
30. Bynner JM, Ferri E, Shepherd P et al, 1997, *Twenty Somethings in the 1990s: Getting on, betting by, getting nowhere*, Aldgate Press, Basingstoke.
31. Gregg P and Wadsworth J, 1998, *Unemployment and Non-Employment: Unpacking economic inactivity*, EPI.
32. *The Real Deal: What young people really think about government, politics and social exclusion*, Demos, London, 1999.
33. Wilkinson H, 1996, 'New kids on the block' in *The Return of the Local*, Demos Quarterly 9, Demos, London.
34. Gregg P, 1999, 'The Impact of Unemployment and Job Loss on Future Earnings' in *Persistent Poverty and Lifetime Inequality: The evidence*, Case Report 5, London, 95.
35. Klerman JA and Karoly LA, 1995, *The Transition to Stable Employment: The experience of US youth in their early labour market career*, National Center for Research in Vocational Education, Berkeley, California; Schroder L, 'Dead end jobs and upgrading plans: an evaluation of Job Creation Programmes' in Wadensjo E, ed, 1996, *The Nordic Labour Markets in the 1990s, Part 2*, Elsevier, Amsterdam; OECD, 1997, *The OECS Employment Outlook: Low wage jobs: Stepping Stones or Traps?*, The OECD Observer no 208, Organisation for Economic Cooperation and Development, Paris.
36. Whereas in 1979, just 4.9 per cent of men with no qualifications were economically inactive, in 1997, the figure had risen to

28.7 per cent. Figures from.Gregg and Wadsworth, 1998 (note 31).

37. Ianni, F, The Search for Structure: a report on American Youth Today (New York, Free Press, 1989)

38. Comprehensive Spending Review, 1998 (see note 14)

39. Bynner J [unpublished paper], 'Origins of Social Exclusion: Risk factors affecting young children'.

40. Littlewood J and Botting B, 1998, 'Which children are "at risk" and where are they?' in Comprehensive Spending Review (see note 14).

41. Select Committee on Education and Employment Fifth Report, section A, The Stationary Offic,. London, 1998. See also Graham and Bowling for profiles of young offenders.

42. See note 41.

43. Taking risks: an analysis of the risks of homelessness for young people in London, A report for Safe in the City, London, 1999.

44. See note 43.

45. Social exclusions in Milton Keynes: towards a multi-agency strategy, The final report of the prevention and family support network, Milton Keynes Council, April 1998.

46. Social Exclusion Unit, 1998, Bringing Britain Together: A national Strategy for neighbourhood renewal, The Stationary Office, London.

47. See note 40.

48. Bynner J, 1998, 'Education and family components of identity in the transition from school to work' in International Journal of Behavioural Development, no 22.

49. Evidence on risk factors : Rutter M, 1990, 'Psychosocial resilience and protective mechanisms' in Rolf J, Masten AS, Cicchetti D et al, Risk and Protective Factors in the Development of Psychopathology; Garmezy N, 1985, 'Stress-resistent children: the search for protective factors' in Stevenson JE, ed, Recent Research in Developmental Psychopathology, book supplement to the Journal of Child Pyschology and Pschiatry 4, 213-233. Garmezy N, 1987, The Invulnerable Child, Guilford Press, New York; Bempechat J, 1998, Against the Odds: how 'at-risk' students exceed expectations, Jossey-Bass, San Fransisco; Tierney JP, Grossman JB, Resch NL, 1995, Making A Difference: An impact study of Big Brothers/Big Sisters, Public/Private Ventures, Philadelphia.

50. The idea for this schema came originally from Professor David Hargreaves of the University of Cambridge.

51. 6, P, 1998, The Future of Privacy, volume 1: Private Life and Public Policy, Demos London.

52. Gambone MA and Arbreton AJA, 1997, Safe Havens: The contributions of youth organisations to healthy adolescent development, Public/Private Ventures, Philadelphia.

53. See note 32.

54. Research, Policy and Practice Forum on Young People, 1999, Creating Dialogue and Improving Links: The report of the launch of the forum, Youth Work Press, Leicester.

55. Ferguson RF, Clay PL et al, 1996, YouthBuild in Developmental Perspective: A formative evaluation of the YouthBuild Demonstration Project, MIT, Cambridge, Massachusetts.

56. Tiernen, Crossman and Resch, 1995 (note 49).

57. Dusseldorp Skills Forum, 1998, Australia's Youth: Reality and risk, Dusseldorp Skills Forum, Sydney.

58. Jobs for the Future, 1999, Business Participation in Welfare-to-Work: Lessons from the United States, Jobs for the Future, Boston, Massachusetts.

59. Pettit B, ed, 1999, Children and Work in the UK: Reassessing the issues, Child Poverty Action Group, London

60. Gardner H, 1999, The Disciplined Mind, Simon and Schuster, New York.

61. Pearce N and Hillman J, 1998, Wasted Youth: Raising achievement, tackling exclusion, IPPR, London.

62. Meagher N, 1998, Empoyability: The views of empoyers on Tynside, Tameside TEC Ltd.

63. DfEE/NYA, 1998, England's Youth Service: The 1998 audit, Youth Work Press, Leicester.

64. Ianni F, 1989, The Search for Structure: a report on American youth today, The Free Press, New York.

65. Damon W, 1997, The Youth Charter, The Free Press, New York.

66. DETR, 1998, Where Does Public Spending Go? Pilot study to analyse the flows of public expenditure into local areas,DETR, London.

67. Kemple J, 1997, Career Academies: Communities of Support for Students and Teachers: Further findings from a ten-site evaluation, Manpower Demonstration Research Corporation, Washington DC.

68. OECD, 1996, Lifelong Learning For All, Organisation for Economic Cooperation and Development, Paris.